The Way

— OF —

SAINT
JAMES

The Way
— OF —
SAINT
JAMES

A PILGRIMAGE TO
SANTIAGO DE COMPOSTELA

James Bentley

Photographs by John Miller

PAVILION

First published in Great Britain in 1992 by
PAVILION BOOKS LIMITED
196 Shaftesbury Avenue, London WC2H 8JL

A CIP record for this book is available from the British Library.

ISBN 1 85145 399 7
10 9 8 7 6 5 4 3 2 1

Filmset by SX Composing Ltd, Rayleigh, Essex
Printed and bound in Great Britain by The Bath Press

I should very much like to express my gratitude to Jennifer Paton,
Marketing Director of the Magic of Italy, 227 Shepherd's Bush Road,
London W6 7AS, and to her colleague Katherine Mitchell, who arranged
for me to spend some time at the Hotel Riosol, Avenida Palencia 3, Leon.

Contents

INTRODUCTION

A T THE HEIGHT of its popularity during the middle ages an estimated 500 thousand pilgrims (some authorities calculate more) arrived annually at the shrine of St. James the Great in Santiago de Compostela. Though many of them travelled on horseback, more journeyed on foot, covering some sixteen kilometres an hour. They did so in spite of warnings of the dangers on the way. Aimery Picaud, the most authoritative medieval guide, was especially wary of the inhabitants of Navarra, describing them as 'perverse, perfidious, disloyal, corrupt, voluptuous, expert in every violence, cruel and quarrelsome.' For good measure he added that 'any one of them would murder a pilgrim for a sou.'

Apart from the Spaniards themselves, these pilgrims for the most part came from the Low Countries, from Britain, from Germany, from Italy, from Portugal and from France. They set out from their own pilgrimage centres, many of which had intimate connections with St. James the Great of Spain. Reading Abbey, for instance, displayed what was reputed to be one of his arms. Again, in the mid-twelfth century the Count of Ferrette returned from a pilgrimage to Santiago de Compostela to his home near Feldbach, close by the Swiss frontier in the Sundgau, and founded there a Cistercian abbey dedicated to St. James the Great. One of the purposes of this book is to explore a string of similar architectural masterpieces which were built along the pilgrimage route.

If we are to trust Dante, the fame of Santiago de Compostela rose as far as heaven itself. In the twenty-fifth canto of the *Paradiso* the poet meets the saint:

> *Indi si mosse un lume verso noi*
> *di quella spera ond'uscì la primizia*
> *che lasciò Cristo de'vicari suoi.*
> *E la mia donna piena di letizia,*
> *mi disse: 'Mira, mira: ecco il barone*
> *per cui laggiù si visita Galizia!'*

(Then out of the crowd from which had come
   the first fruits of Christ's earthly vicars
   a light moved towards us.
Seeing it my Lady, filled with joy
   cried to me 'Lo! Lo!: behold the noble one
   who makes galicia throng with visitors.')

How St. James the Great made Galicia throng with visitors is another of the themes of this book. To answer that question involves legends as well as history, particularly those concerned with the re-covery of Spain from Moorish rule and the role of St. James (as the country's patron saint) in this reconquest. Other half-legendary, half-historical figures also play their part in the story, including the Emperor Charlemagne and his champions Roland and Oliver.

Eventually Santiago de Compostela matched Jerusalem and Rome in its power to attract pilgrims. Many who never made the journey, such as St. Francis of Assisi, were reputed to have done so. And the pilgrimage survived both the Reformation and the age of scepticism. Over four thousand people were annually arriving at the shrine by the end of the 1980s. The visit of Pope John Paul II in 1989 more than doubled that number. A papal bull of 1179 had established the years in which the feast of St. James falls on a Sunday as Jubilee years, and these today still swell the stream of pilgrims.

Modern pilgrims to Santiago de Compostela travel on foot, by bicycle, on horseback, by vanload or by car (which has been my own custom). A considerable number drive as far as Roncesvalles in the Pyrenees and walk the rest of the way, hiking some 700 kilometres. At 25 kilometres a day (for roads have improved since the middle ages) their journey lasts about a month. Although the Spanish tourist authorities have taken to signposting the route, medieval pilgrims would often deviate from the well-trodden paths, and that is what I recommend as I recount my own pilgrimage, for the footprints of St. James have marked some entrancing spots well-off the beaten track.

From outside Spain four traditional pilgrimage routes reach Santiago de Compostela from France alone – one from Arles in Provence, another from Le Puy in the Auvergne, a third from Véze-lay in Burgundy and the fourth from Paris itself. Every other route from north-west Europe inevitably passed through Paris, and Paris is where I start my own pilgrimage.

CHAPTER ONE

FROM PARIS TO AN EMPTY TOMB

PARIS – SCEAUX – LONGJUMEAU – ANTONY – MONTHLÉRY – ETRÉCHY –
ORLÉANS – LA CHAPELLE-SAINT-MESMIN – MEUNG-SUR-LOIRE – CLÉRY-
SAINT-ANDRÉ – BEAUGENCY – VENDÔME – FRÉTEVAL – LAVARDIN –
SAINT-JACQUES-DES-GUÉRETS – TOURS.

HUMBLE RUE SAINT-JACQUES is almost certainly the oldest street in Paris. Still straight enough to match our favourite image of a Roman road, the street, so scholars say, even pre-dates the Roman conquest of Gaul. The conquerors turned a Gaulish track into Via Superior.

I wish I could add that it runs directly from the square Saint-Jacques, but just south of the square rue Saint-Jacques has been renamed rue de la Cité. In this square rises one of the most elegant Gothic belfries in Paris. Situated at the central crossroads of medieval Paris, the tour Saint-Jacques once belonged to a church which in one form or another has stood here since the days of the Emperor Charlemagne.

Standing in this square Saint-Jacques and about to begin a pilgrimage which would take me to Santiago de Compostela in Spain, I asked myself whether my parents, when they baptized me James, thought they were dedicating me to Jesus's apostle Saint James the Great. Probably not, for they were English presbyterians, and my father was also called James, as was my grandfather and his father too. To be baptized James was a family tradition. Still, when I came to be confirmed I took care to arrange for this to happen on 25 July, the feast of St James the Great. Now I was gazing at one of the loveliest church towers in Paris, a magnificent belfry dedicated to my patron saint.

Save for the press of pilgrims passing through Paris from Britain, from the Low Countries, from Germany and from northern France, the church of Saint-Jacques-de-la-Boucherie would still have been dedicated to St Martin of Tours. No other church in Paris had been consecrated to St James. But as the rumour spread that the corpse of St James the Great had been discovered in Spain and was on display to pilgrims, the canny custodians of this church soon profited from its position on the main artery through Paris, changed its name to Saint-Jacques and soon began to attract increasing numbers of the pilgrims (and the financial rewards they brought) who were passing through the city on their way to Spain.

Why anyone should suppose that the body of St James the Great is to be found in Spain is a tricky question. Nothing in the Bible, which is our only authentic source of information about him, indicates this. Born in Galilee, he was a fisherman summoned as a disciple by Jesus, when his Lord discovered him mending nets along with his brother John and his father Zebedee. His nickname 'the Great' distinguised this saint from another, presumably smaller disciple of Jesus who was also named James. The two brothers, James and John, became members of Jesus's inner ring of disciples. Because of their fiery tempers Jesus gave them the nickname *Boanarges*, which means 'sons of thunder'. In spite of this inherent wildness, both brothers professed themselves willing to die in the service of Jesus, and St James the Great was the first to follow his master in this way. In AD 44 King Herod Agrippa I, in order to please the Jewish enemies of the new Christian sect, began to persecute the followers of Jesus. The book of the Acts of the Apostles simply records that Agrippa killed James, the brother of John, with the sword.

So the decapitated body of the apostle presumably lay entombed in Jerusalem. Then, around the year 810, Bishop Theodomir of Irinese, whose see lay in the north-west corner of Spain, claimed that, guided by a star, a hermit named Pelayo had discovered St James's corpse in the wild countryside of his diocese, buried alongside two of his disciples. King Alfonso II of Asturia and Leon welcomed the discovery of the apostle's tomb, and built a sanctuary over it. The place became known as St James of the field of the Star, or Santiago de Compostela (though dusty philologists sometimes contest the derivation from the Latin *campus stellae* and insist the Compostela derives from the word for a place of burial, *compositum*).

Legends blossomed in order to support the authenticity of the relics. Before his martyrdom St James, it was said, had preached the Christian gospel in Spain. After his burial in Jerusalem his relics had been exhumed, placed in an unmanned ship and sailed of their own accord to Spain, landing in the realms of a pagan queen named Lupa. A further twist to the legend declared that a horseman, following the ship on the shore, fell into the water and drowned. The apostle brought him back to life, and he emerged from the sea covered in scallop shells – henceforth one of the emblems of the saint and of the pilgrims who came to visit his shrine.

Then the tale became all the more complex and marvellous because of the Muslim conquest of Spain and its gradual reconquest by the Christians. The Moors invaded from North Africa in 711. After defeating the Christians they remained for the most part tolerant masters, for their underlings were also 'people of the book', sharing with Muslims those scriptures which Christians dub the Old Testament. Occasionally Muslim warlords such as El Mansour would ravage Christian cities, but such occurrences were rare. Yet in the face of these heathen conquests and depradations, visions of St James rallied the Christian forces. In 844 at the battle of Clajivo in the Ebro valley he was said to have appeared at the side of King Ramiro 1 on a white charger, brandishing his sword and rallying the Christian troops as they defeated the Moors. Estimates varied as to the number of Muslims the saint decapitated.

In real life the sons of thunder displayed a thirst for vengeance. One of the Gospels (Luke chapter 9, verses 52 to 54) tells us that Jesus once sent messengers to some villagers to arrange for them to receive him, but they refused. When James and John saw this they said to Jesus, 'Lord, do you want us to bid fire come down from heaven and consume them?' But the Gospel tells us that Jesus rebuked them both for this bloodthirsty suggestion. By the year 844 it seems that the rebuke had been forgotten. St James the Great had been transformed into Santiago Matamoros, St James the Moor-slayer, patron saint of Christian Spain. And in 1488, before the troops of King Ferdinand and Queen Isabella of Spain finally expelled the Moors from their realm, the two Catholic sovereigns came to Compostela to kneel before the relics of St James and beg his aid.

So the 'son of thunder' developed from a disciple of Jesus and possible author of one of the books of the New Testament in to a pilgrim saint, whose other guise was that of slayer of Moors. Statues and paintings of St James often depict him carrying the New Testament epistle which bears his name. Ironically, the letter of St James re inforces what he called the 'royal law', namely, 'You shall love your neighbour as yourself.' James went on to declare that 'the wisdom from above is first pure, then peaceable, gentle, open to reason, full of mercy and good fruits'. Muslims seemed to have been outside the scope of this wisdom and this royal law.

As pilgrims flocked to his shrine at Compostela, countless hospices, churches, monasteries and sanctuaries prepared to welcome them on their way. *En route* they would come across both masterpieces and humble works of art in which medieval painters and sculptors depicted St James in one or other of his guises. In 1589, when the English privateer Sir Francis Drake was sailing around Galicia, the cathedral canons decided to hide the saint's corpse. They are then said to have forgotten where they had hidden it. I do not believe this to be true, since pilgrims continued to visit the tomb and some of the more distinguished were allowed to inspect the remains. St James's corpse was more probably lost in the eighteenth century, when the English fleet attacked Galicia during the war of the Spanish succession.

In 1878 the Cardinal Archbishop of Santiago set archaeologists to work to try to find the remains. On the night of 28 January 1879 they found them. Once again the relics were put on display in the cathedral, and in 1884, whatever the scholars might say, a bull of Pope Leo XIII declared that these were the authentic remains of St James the Great. Once again the pilgrimages prospered, with confraternities of St James springing up again throughout Europe. On my own pilgrimage from Paris to Santiago I was to meet several of their members.

Arriving at the central crossroads of medieval Paris, pilgrims came upon the church of St Martin of Tours, which speedily changed its name to Saint-Jacques-de-la-Boucherie. The Carolingian emperors had hardly ever lived at Paris, and the city prospered only when the Capetians, the dynasty founded by Hughes Capet in 987, made it their capital. The subsequent and frequent rebuilding of Saint-Jacques-de-la-Boucherie reflected both this prosperity and also the increasing importance of the pilgrimage to Compostela. At this spot would gather pilgrims from Flanders, Artois and Picardy, from the Low Countries and from Britain.

The anti-clericalists of the French Revolution demolished all but its tower in 1797. Looking at it at the start of my own pilgrimage I rejoiced that at least something was spared, for the belfry is a masterpiece of Gothic architecture. Built in the second decade of the sixteenth century to designs by architects who included two brilliant brothers, Jean and Didier de Felin, it carries on one of its north-west pinnacles a massive statue of St James himself. Since there are only four pinnacles capable of carrying other such statues, the architects evidently decided to replace one of the four evangelists, St John, with the statue of the saint of Compostela, setting on the other pinnacles statues of a bull, a lion and an eagle (symbols respectively of St Luke, St Mark and St Matthew). The tour Saint-Jacques fairly bristles with other statues, the most significant being that of Blaise Pascal, who climbed the tower in 1648 to carry out his celebrated barometrical experiments. Fittingly, I suppose, the top of the belfry is a meteorological station, but when I asked permission to climb it myself I was told that this is not allowed.

The church of Saint-Jacques-de-la-Boucherie is incidentally not the only victim of senseless destruction to be commemorated in this square. Here too is a medallion of the poet Gérard de Nerval, sculpted by Jehan du Seigneur in 1851. Four years later de Nerval hanged himself from a nearby lamp-post.

Few can resist browsing among those curious bookstalls set near here on the banks of the River Seine, and there I had a stroke of good fortune of the kind which blessed me throughout the whole of my journey to Compostela, for I picked up a 1954 issue of the monthly review *Plaisir de France* containing a couple of fascinating pages about the very belfry I had just been admiring. The article was concerned with that curious architectural and mathematical formula, the golden section. Though this aesthetically remarkable ratio was first precisely formulated in the fifteenth century by an Italian Renaissance mathematician named Lucas Pacioli, the golden section has been used as a measure of architectural proportion since antiquity. Pacioli defined it as the division of a line in which the ratio of the shorter section to the longer is the same as that of the longer section to the whole, i.e approximately that of 5 to 8 and of 8 to 13. The piece in *Plaisir de France* illustrated the use of this proportion in the columns of the Parthenon, in the so-called royal portal of Chartres cathedral, in Titian's painting *Sacred and Profane Love* and Michelangelo's portrait of the Holy Family, in the proportions of the human finger and finally in the tour Saint-Jacques. So I walked back to the square Saint-Jacques for another look at the belfry. The article is absolutely correct: tour Saint-Jacques is built according to the golden section – and in a most complex and intriguing fashion. The proportions of the buttresses of the tower illustrate the golden section upwards, so to speak, growing shorter as they rise. The top two sections relate to each other according to Pacioli's mathematical rule, and so do the bottom two sections. Then the three sets of windows illustrate the same proportions, only downwards, for this time they grow longer as they rise. Yet still the bottom two and the top two relate to each other according to Pacioli's formula.

Having thus – in part at any rate – explained the aesthetic theory behind the beauty of the tour Saint-Jacques, it was time for me to start the pilgrimage. Rue de la Cité is one of the most favoured in Paris. Pilgrims then and now would cross the Pont-Notre-Dame, as I did, to the Ile de la Cité. It was Sunday, and a small open-air market was in full swing, selling flowers and herbs and caged birds. Close by the medieval Hôtel-Dieu of Paris I spotted a statuesque bronze group, sculpted in the 1880s and representing Charlemagne accompanied by his knights Roland and Oliver. Whoever commissioned these statues was imaginative, for the three men, as we shall see, soon began to play their part in the mythology of Compostela.

The *Chanson de Roland*, which tells the heroic tale of Roland, Oliver and their companions, was written around 1100 and is the earliest of the so-called *chansons de geste*, a remarkable group of epic poems about the struggles of Christian France against the Muslims. In them Charlemagne is portrayed as the hero of the struggle, along with his court of twelve noble peers who include as well as Roland and Oliver a Dane named Ogier and Archbishop Turpin.

Of course these poems cannot be relied on for historical accuracy about events occurring some four centuries or more before they were written. None the less they each contain some historical core. The death of Roland and Oliver did take place in the Roncesvalles pass in the province of Navarre in northern Spain, after Charlemagne's army had ravaged Pamplona in 778. Roland and Oliver perished when the rearguard of the army was ambushed by Basques. In the *Chanson de Roland* all this has been transformed into a heroic last stand against the Saracen. Charlemagne is represented as having conquered almost all Spain, while the Saracen king is suing for peace. At Roland's request, so the *Chanson* continues, his stepfather Ganelon is sent to negotiate the terms. The task is a dangerous one, and the treacherous Ganelon decides to destroy the one who suggested him as envoy. On his return from the negotiations he ensures that Roland will command the rear of the army. Surrounded by a massive force of Saracens, Roland is urged by Oliver to sound his horn and summon help from the French army. Too proud to do so until it is too late, Roland perishes, along with his peers and soldiers.

Though it contains no hint of the pilgrimage to Santiago de Compostela, from the twelfth century onwards few pilgrims at this point in their journey would have resisted entering the cathedral of Notre-Dame which Maurice de Sully, Bishop of Paris, began building in 1160. The Notre-Dame we revere today is a somewhat different building. By the time Victor Hugo came to eulogize it in 1831 as 'a vast symphony of stone' and 'a human creation as powerful and fecund as the divine creation', the cathedral was in a sorry state, dilapidated by time and neglect and even pillaged by mobs. A sum of 2,650,000 francs was entrusted to the arthitects Lassus and Viollet-le-Duc to restore it. Since Lassus died in 1857 and the work was not finally completed till 1864, the Gothic fantasy we see today is largely Viollet-le-Duc's own re-creation of a medieval cathedral. He had, incidentally, spent a further six million francs before his work was accomplished.

I walked from here across the Petit-Pont and on to join peaceful rue Saint-Jacques. Paris is quiet on Sunday mornings, and as I crossed rue Soufflet and looked left towards the Panthéon I imagined the illustrious dead inside it even deeper in sleep than usual. In the past pilgrims to Compostela would be reminded of their purpose by passing through the city ramparts by way of a partly thirteenth-, partly fourteenth-century gate named the porte Saint-Jacques, but today we have to make do with a plaque on the wall of number 772 reminding us that it once stood here. Some of the houses in this neighbourhood are venerable. Echoes of the route to Compostela reappear in the names of the rue des Fossés-Saint-Jacques, which my road crossed, and of the church of Saint-Jacques-de-Haut-Pas, situated where in the thirteenth century a group of Hospitallers (known as *les Hospitaliers d'Alto Passo*) had set up a pilgrims' hospice.

Shortly I was in the faubourg Saint-Jacques and my street had become the rue du Faubourg-Saint-Jacques. So I found my car and left Paris, still following this ancient axis of the city until it reached the N20 on the way to Etampes. I find this an extremely boring road, and was happy to escape from it as soon as possible, for even today an industrial suburb like Bagneaux retains a pretty thirteenth-century church, while a little further south Sceaux is an exquisite oasis. The parish church of Saint-Jean-Baptiste was founded in 1203 by the bishop of Paris, Eudes de Sully. Here in the seventeenth century Le Nôtre and his successors designed a magnificante park for Jean Baptise-Colbert, who had inherited a fortune from his father in 1683 and had also grown personally rich as a courtier and as secretary of state for the French navy.

In neither spot, however, did I discover any direct reference either to St James or to Compostela. We do know that pilgrims did pass through the town of Antony a little further south on the way to Longjumeau, for here stood a commandery of the Knights Templar which once sheltered pilgrims to Compostela. This was the first of many such hospices on my way to Compostela. The Templars had been founded in the Holy Land around the year 1120 by a group of French knights led by Hugues de Payens. Their initial aim was to protect pilgrims to Jerusalem from the attacks of bands of Muslims. Deeply devout, at first they were widely acclaimed. King Baldwin II of Jerusalem gave them official quarters in part of the royal palace, which occupied the site of the former Jewish Temple (hence the name by which the knights came to be known). No less a saint than Bernard of Clairvaux wrote a rule of life for the order, and their fame, numbers and influence rapidly increased.

Throughout Europe they acquired and built vast properties as well as hospices, still commited to caring for and escorting pilgrims, still ready to fight against the infidel. But in the early fourteenth century their overweening power alarmed King Philip IV, the Fair, of France. He also coveted their wealth. Whether on trumped up charges or not, the Templars were accused both of immorality and of heresy. In 1312 the King managed to persuade Pope Clement V to suppress the order. Two years later the grand master of the Templars, Jacques de Molay, was burnt at the stake.

At Longjumeau I asked to see their commandery and was instantly directed to some ruins beside a stream known as the Rouillon. Apart from a thirteenth-century bridge, all that remains here from the Middle Ages is a lovely church dedicated to St Martin of Tours, founded in the thirteenth century and rebuilt two hundred years later. Since the ultimate aim of the pilgrimage was to venerate the human remains of St James the Great, relics littering the way were additional treats. Churches collected them enthusiastically, in part simply to ensure that pilgrims paid a visit. Saint-Martin-de-Tours at Longjumeau boasts no fewer than four such relics: a piece of its patron saint, a bone of St Louis (King of France and pilgrim to Compostela, who died on a crusade in 1270), St Vincent de Paul (whose birthplace lies further on our way), and finally even a piece of the true Cross. They are still there.

Another fine church at Antony is Saint-Saturnin, dating back to the thirteenth century, but ravaged during the Hundred Years' War and rebuilt in the fifteenth century. Louis IV established a beeswax factory here in 1703. Today the factory serves as a convent, but you can identify it by a sculpted emblem on its wall, depicting a beehive with the quaint motto, 'They work for God and the King' (*Deo regique laborant*).

Although I was not making much progress, I was greatly enjoying these neglected spots in the environs of Paris, and decided not to hurry on but to stay the night at Etampes, scarcely a dozen kilometres south. On the way lies Monthléry, once dominated by a powerful medieval citidel of which but the keep remains. More redolent of the past is the thirteenth-century doorway of its hospital (which was founded in 1149). The inscription over the doorway declares that it was founded by Louis VII, the King of France who not only launched the disastrous second crusade but also divorced his wife, Eleanor of Aquitaine – with the result that she instantly married Henry II of England and thus occasioned the long and dreadful wars over her patrimony.

Etréchy, on the left bank of the River Juine, was the scene of my penultimate pause before finding a bed for the night at Etampes. Philogists impropably derive the name Etréchy from *strata via*, the name of the Roman road which bisects the village and which saw the tramp of many a medieval pilgrim. Today the chief delight of Etréchy is the splendid twelfth-century church of Saint-Etienne, enriched inside with sculpted capitals. From here I walked a couple of kilometres west to Chauffour-lès-Etréchy, looking for another pilgrims' hospice. Until 1307 it was run by the Knights Templar. In that year the commandery of this doomed order was taken over by the Knights Hospitaller, yet another order devoted to the care of pilgrims. Founded a century before the Templars, the Hospitallers were destined long to outlast them. Their name derives from a hospital for sick pilgrims, set up in the eleventh century close by the church of St John the Baptist in Jerusalem. (In consequence these Hospitallers were also often called the Knights of St John of Jerusalem). When the crusaders captured Jerusalem in 1099, the hospital superior, a monk named Gérard, took the opportunity of expanding the work, starting similar hospitals on the pilgrim routes to Jerusalem both from France and from Italy.

Crusaders who had benefited from the care of the Hospitallers bestowed lands on the order, sometimes even becoming members themselves, pledged not only to look after the sick and the poor but also to fight against the Muslims. The Muslims fought back, and when in 1291 they took Acre from the Christians, the Hospitallers left the Holy Land to continue their work from Europe and Cyprus. Twenty years later the Hospitallers, by now a naval power, acquired Rhodes (and yet another name, the Knights of Rhodes). The Turks took it from them in 1522, but the Emperor Charles v gave them a new base, Malta, and with it a new name, the Knights of Malta. Only when Napoleon Bonaparte took Malta from them in 1798 did the Hospitallers cease to be a territorial power – though they continued to be a body devoted to charity and the care of the sick and poor.

At Chauffour-lès-Etréchy you can still see a few vestiges of their hospice, including some granite markers inscribed with the Maltese cross. More rewarding visually is the lovely church which the members of this charitable order founded, the eleventh and thirteenth-century Saint-Jean. Inside I discovered a twelfth-century tomb. Then I walked back to Etréchy and drove on to Etampes.

As you approach Etampes the N20 ceases to be boring. Undoubtedly the best initial way to savour the town is to drive past it for a glimpse from the road of the remarkable leaning tower of the church of Saint-Martin. Then you can turn off the N20 and arrive at the oldest part of the town, which surrounds this church. Saint-Martin is not the oldest church to have stood on this spot, but it is venerable enough. Begun by Benedictine monks in the mid-twelfth century, its style, beginning with the Romanesque apse, progresses towards the west end through a Gothic choir and nave as far as the Renaissance belfry, which was finished in 1537. Apparently it began to lean the moment it was built, and you can see how the builders attempted to straighten it further up. A leaning tower that has not fallen down for nearly five centuries might well be trusted to stay up a little longer. It even carries three great bells; but I still preferred to park my car closer to the apse.

This is a pilgrims' church – though intended as much for devotees of St Martin of Tours as for those of St James of Compostela. The pilgrimage to Compostela has however left its mark on this church. In fact Santiago de Compostela must bear responsibility for a major shift in European ecclesiastical architecture, for the design of the churches and cathedrals on the pilgrimage routes were frequently adapted simply to cope with the countless men and women who thronged their pavements. Their long naves were now flanked by wide aisles, so as to allow the crowds to be marshalled more easily. These aisles led to a deambulatory, a passageway around the semicircular apse of the church which took the pilgrims behind the high altar, where they could walk from one chapel to another, each one housing the relics of Christian saints enclosed in exquisite shrines.

In the greatest of these churches, in the middle of the church, a more or less isolated section allowed the clergy to continue chanting their daily offices, virtually oblivious to the mass of pilgrims who often threatened to overwhelm the rest of the church. Often the aisles were built with a second storey, to be filled with pilgrims when there was no room for them on the ground floor. The four finest such buildings on the pilgrimage route were Saint-Martin at Tours, Saint-Martial at Limoges, Sainte-Foy at Conques and the mighty cathedral of Compostela itself.

The church of Saint-Martin at Etampes is a humbler example of this adaptation of church design to serve the needs of the medieval pilgrim, for it is the sole one in the town to possess a deambulatory, enabling the devout to proceed in an orderly fashion around the east end, passing behind the high altar and paying their respects to the various relics on display in the chapels radiating from it. Though St Martin of Tours did have prime position here, one of the chapels housed a statue of St James which has been stolen.

In the right aisle I was much taken by a tombstone, dating I think from the mid-thirteenth century and depicting the Blessed Virgin Mary standing on the moon. This most curious image was beloved by medieval sculptors, for they assimilated the mother of Jesus with one of the visions of the Apocalypse of St John the Divine, who described 'a great portent in heaven, a woman clothed with the sun, with the moon under her feet, and on her head a crown of twelve stars'. The Apolcalypse continues, 'She was with child and she cried out in her pangs of birth, in anguish for delivery. And another portent appeared in heaven: behold, a great red dragon, with seven heads and ten horns, and seven diadems upon his head. His tail swept down a third of the stars of heaven, and cast them to the earth. And the dragon stood before the woman who was about to bear a child, that he might devour it when she brought it forth; she brought forth a male child, one who is to rule all the nations with a rod of iron, but her child was caught up to God and to his throne.'

So a little medieval tomb took me back into the wildness of Biblical apolcalyptic. Then I drove into the centre of the town and found myself a bed and some food at the hotel Au Duc d'Orléans. In Paris it is wise to unload a car completely before leaving it overnight outside a hotel. Etampes is thirty-five kilometres from Paris and the hotel had no secure parking, so I asked the landlord whether the contents of my car were safe. 'Safe from the people of Etampes, but possibly not from Parisians who might be passing by,' he replied. All I was worried about was my word processor, so he kindly stored it for me in the wine-cellar.

Wine turned out to preoccupy me for most of the evening, since I shared a table not with pilgrims but with a M. and Mme Bannwarth, who are wine merchants from Obermorschwihr in Alsace. Much of the wine drunk in Paris, they explained, comes from this northerly wine-growing region of France, which is why they were here to do business. Only a fool (such as myself) shows off his minimal knowledge to an expert, but they let me get away with haltingly quoting an Alsatian wine proverb: 'If I drink, I stumble and limp, but if I don't drink, I limp none the less. Why not drink and limp, rather than limp sober?' (which in the bizarre Alsatian patois runs *Trink i, so hink i. Trink i net so hink i doch. Liewer trinke und hinke, als nit trinke und doch hinke*). Hubris brought its fall when I observed that in my view wines from Alsace are in general dearer than wines from other parts of France. M. Bannwarth patiently explained that better wines are mostly dearer; inferior wines are mostly cheaper.

One virtue of the Hôtel Au Duc d'Orléans is that it stands opposite the superb Romanesque church of Notre-Dame-du-Fort, which was founded in the eleventh century and rebuilt in part some five times. The Romanesque statues of the south porch were all mutilated by Protestants in 1562 during the wars of religion, yet the swirls of their sculpted clothing remain exquisite. The statues all sit on what seem to me little wicker chairs, while two angels with thuribles cense the Christ figure. Notre-Dame-du-Fort boasts simple rose windows and a graceful spire with little three-storey turrets at each corner. Its west porch is also sculpted with scenes from the Nativity. Though again mutilated, it is easy to make out the angel announcing to Mary that she shall conceive a child. Next to this scene Mary lies in bed, her newly-born baby lying in swaddling clothes in a cradle. Then the porch portrays the massacre of the innocents on the orders of King Herod. Finally Mary flees on a donkey with her son to Egypt.

The interior is magnificently unruly, the result of successive re-buildings, with even the floor on different levels. The finest statues inside, to my mind, are the Romanesque ones of St Peter and St Paul, in the chapel on the left of the high altar. St James himself does appear in this church, in a painting behind the statue of the Virgin Mary over the tympanum of the north doorway. But I think I detected here another quaint, almost covert reference to the crusades and to St James's mythical role in the medieval struggle between Christendom and Islam. Over the sacristy door is a wall painting of 1514 depicting the choice made by a Jerusalem mob between the murderer Barabbas and Jesus at the request of the Roman procurator Pontius Pilate. Pilate presents Jesus to the people with the words 'Ecce Homo'. The mob shouts back 'Not him. Barabbas.' So, weakly, Pilate condemns Jesus to an unjust death. The anonymous artist has portrayed him not as a Roman but in a turban.

I visited the tiny crypt of the church and then left to stroll around the rest of the town. Etampes is filled with white stone buildings and with narrow cobbled streets, some of them still drained by a gulley down the middle. Gothic and Renaissance homes, some with little turrets, still grace the town. In 1537 King François I of France decided to please the husband of his mistress, Anne de Pisseleu, by making him Duke of Etampes, and the following year an extremely elegant Renaissance house was built for her here. When the King died, Anne de Pisseleu lost favour at court, and Diane de Poitiers, mistress of Henri II, replaced her as Duchess of Etampes. She brought the sculptor Jean Goujon from Paris in 1554 to build the Hôtel de Diane de Poitiers, which rivals in charm the house of Anne de Pisseleu.

In 1589, tired of being the object of envious invasions by Germans and then by English, the citizens themselves demanded that the fuedal château and the medieval fortifications be dismantled, so that Etampes would no longer seem such a great prize. As a result we cannot today walk into the town, as pilgrims to Compostela did till then, through the ancient gate of Saint-Jacques. The ruins of the château above the town, including the twelfth-century keep known as the tour de Guinette, make me regret its demolition. The keep itself resisted, and barrels of gunpowder inside it failed to demolish it entirely. In consequence in 1772 Canon Desforges, an intrepid clergy-man and pioneer of aviation, was able to jump of it in a feather-covered wicker basket, hoping to fly. He fell straight to the ground, but escaped with a bruised elbow.

I walked from the place de l'Hôtel de Ville up past the two homes of the long-dead royal mistresses towards the massive belfry of the church of Saint-Basile. Founded around 1120, the west doorway of the church is decorated with a Romanesque Last Judgement. This church was built in the twelfth century by Hospitallers, and to my delight, a notice was affixed to the railings bearing the words *Chemin de Saint-Jacques*, and decorated with cockle-shells and a couple of pilgrims' staffs and bags. The notice added that the building is today a centre of Compostelan studies. Unfortunately, throughout my whole time at Etampes it remained resolutely locked.

I sought comfort in a bookshop, whose proprietor sold me a locally produced pamphlet on the subject of the pilgrims to Santiago de Compostela, written by an Etampes history teacher named Michael Billard. One of those delicious ragbags that local historians so pleasingly produce, the work is far more concerned with the un-sung delights of Etampes than it is with St James the Great. But it contains one remarkable nugget of information, namely that Etampes was once a staging-post on a route to Compostela from Germany. Michael Billard produced two pieces of evidence for this. First, in the chapel of an old people's home in rue de Gérofosse is a piece of bone from the patroness of Cologne, St Ursula.

I have in fact seen her skull. This legendary woman, along with eleven noble virgins, each accompanied by a thousand attendant vir-gins, travelled on foot to meet the Pope in Rome, returned to Cologne, and are reputed to have been massacred by Huns in AD 238. Buried in a Roman cemetery, their sacred remains were discovered in 1106 and now are displayed in an extraordinary chapel, the so-called Golden Chamber attached to the church of Sankt Ursula, Cologne.

In a glass case on the altar resides the little skull of Ursula herself. On all four walls of this chapel thousands and thousands of other bones are arranged in brilliantly inventive patterns. As Byron im-politely put it, the relics of these virgins include:

> Eleven thousand maidenheads of bone,
>
> The greatest number flesh has ever known.

Somehow, presumably brought by a German pilgrim, a piece of St Ursula herself reached Etampes.

The author of the pamphlet about Etampes and the pilgrimage road to Compostela has dug deeper into history and discovered that on 15 May 1786 a group of German pilgrims reached Guillerval, a few kilometres south of Etampes. There one of them gave birth to a daughter. On the same day she was baptized Anne-Catherine by the local parish priest. The father was named Joseph Vacher, his wife was Gertrude Comerin, and the parish priest recorded in his register that they came from the Electorate of Trier and were on their way to Santiago de Compostela. The priest added that both the godfather and the godmother also came from Trier, and that the latter could not sign her name.

It was time to leave Etampes, by way of the one visible reminder of the old pilgrimage route to Compostela, rue Saint-Jacques, which once ran south from the church of Saint-Basile but has been given a few more names over the centuries. It starts as rue Louis, transforms itself into rue Saint-Jacques and ends as rue Saint-Martin. In rue Saint-Jacques proper rises the town's fourth Romanesque church, Saint-Gilles, which was much damaged when Allied bombers destroyed much of this quarter on 10 June 1944 (killing 150 citizens). The thirteenth-century Gothic steeple of Saint-Gilles withstood the bombardment, and the people of Etampes have restored much of the rest. Saint-Gilles had suffered humiliation before the Second World War, especially after 1792, when the anti-religious faction gained the upper hand during the French Revolution. Transformed first into an assembly room, the church later became a cornmarket.

Through wide green fields the N20 runs on from Etampes to Angerville, where I discovered the late eighteenth-century château of Dommerville and a Gothic church with a Romanesque tower, but no sign of St James. Inside the church, against a pillar facing the font, stands a superb sixteenth-century statue of St John the Baptist. Then I drove on to Orleans.

By a fortunate quirk of history, we still possess a medieval pilgrims' guide-book, written in the twelfth century by a Cluniac monk who lived at Parthenay-le-Vieux, a few kilometres west of Poitiers. His name was Aimery Picaud, and he must surely have followed the pilgrimage routes himself. His five-volume *Liber Sancti Jacobi*, which now belongs to the cathedral of Santiago, recounts the legends surrounding St James the Great, as well as giving much practical information to Picaud's fellow pilgrims. He was writing some twenty years after the composition of the *Chanson de Roland*, and so he included in his work a chronicle describing Charlemagne's forays into Spain and the legendary destruction of his rearguard at the Roncesvalles pass. And the monk cunningly attributed his own work to Pope Callixtus II himself, to give it yet more authority.

Picaud lists four major routes to Compostela, advising pilgrims where they can find lodgings, food and wine, impressive churches and the relics of the great saints. The one by way of Tours he dubbed the 'via turonensis'. Although my intention was broadly to follow it, I determined to wander away from it whenever some enticement beckoned, and in particular not to miss on my way to Spain the shrine at Vézelay, which Picaud placed at the start of his route through Limoges, the 'via lemovicensis'. On no account, he insisted, should any pilgrim on the 'via turonensis' to Compostela miss visiting Orleans cathedral.

The cathedral of Orleans is dedicated to the Holy Cross, and I find it superb, especially the two wedding-cake, seventeenth-century Gothic towers designed by Louis-François Trouard. Under the guidance of Aimery Picaud no pilgrim to Compostela would have failed to attend Mass here, for the guide recounted the story of a miracle which occurred when the fourth-century Bishop of Orleans, St Euvertus, was about to consecrate bread and wine inside his cathedral. As Euvertus traced the sign of the cross over the sacred Host and the chalice, the hand of God appeared over the altar, in full view of the saint and those who were assisting him. Every action of the saint was paralleled by the actions of the divine hand, which also traced the sign of the cross on the elements and raised on high the Host and chalice in time with the same action of Eurvertus. Only when the Mass was over did the hand of God disappear. 'Thus,' Picaud concluded, 'every time a priest sings the Mass, Christ sings it too.'

Much of this fine building had to be rebuilt when the wars of religion ended, for the Huguenots had destroyed most of it. They also threw into the River Loire a statue of the Virgin Mary which since the sixth century had been attracting pilgrims to this city. The city fathers themselves were responsible in the nineteenth century for an act of vandalism which almost obliterated one of the centres of pilgrimage for those on the way to Compostela. In the fifteenth century these pilgrims had paid for a splendid church, built in the flamboyant Gothic style, dedicated to Saint-Jacques and standing close by the old bridge across the river. It was demolished to make way for a covered market. Fortunately the façade and a couple of arcades survived, and in 1883 these were re-erected against a wall in the garden behind what used to be the city's town hall. I found them by walking north from the west end of the cathedral and then left along rue d'Escure into the garden. The remains of the church of Saint-Jacques are exceedingly ornate.

As ever at Orleans I put myself into the Hôtel Moderne (which was modern when it was built in 1902), whose concierge has always proved both amiable and knowledgeable. I dined at a brasserie opposite the railway station, a meal enlivened by some youths who threw a canister of laughing gas through the doorway, forcing us all out on to the pavement. Did pilgrims in former years suffer such assaults? The next morning the concierge of my hotel directed me down rue de la République and rue Royale (where in 1791 William Wordsworth fell in love with Annette Vallon, who became mother of his illegitimate child) as far as the riverside.

At this point by the riverside originally stood the church of Saint-Jacques. But I was looking for the pilgrims' hospice which accompanied it, the *Maison de la Coquille*, the house of the cockle-shell. Hidden away around a corner in the rue de la Pierre-Percée, the façade of this Renaissance hospice was delicately sculpted in the sixteenth century. On its wooden lintel are carved two pilgrims, one carrying a cockle-shell. Perhaps the other also did in the past, but this beautiful *Maison de la Coquille* badly needs restoration, and so I cannot tell.

The next section of my journey was richly rewarded. Crossing the bridge again, I took the N152 in the direction of Blois, stopping after five kilometres at what was once a favoured pilgrimage centre, La Chapelle-Saint-Mesmin. Mesmin was a sixth-century saint whose greatest exploit was to burn a malicious dragon to death by throwing a firebrand at it. For a thousand years his venerable bones were preserved in the church of which he is the patron saint. Pilgrims *en route* to Compostela were among the countless who revered his shrine. Then the Huguenots set the relics of St Mesmin on fire, scattering the ashes in the River Loire. His memorial remains the parish church, built in the eleventh century but incorporating what I judge to be one of the finest pre-Romanesque porches I have seen, built out of stones shaped as clubs and lozenges, and also supported by a couple of beautiful early Romanesque pillars.

My next stop was Meung-sur-Loire, a town filled with flowers and washed by little rivulets. Equally ancient as La Chapelle-Saint-Mesmin, its name, 'meung', derives from two Roman words, 'magus' (which means market) and 'dunum' (which means fortified camp). This was the home of the poet François Villon, who stabbed a priest to death in Paris in 1455 and somehow escaped hanging. Small wonder he adored the blesed Virgin Mary, begging her in his *Ballade poiur prier Notre Dame* to urge her son to absolve him from his many sins. Meung-sur-Loire is still fortified, and the eleventh-century church of Saint-Liphard, in a cruciform shape unusual in this part of France, is a perfect Gothic foil for the basically thirteenth-century château of the Bishops of Orleans. Villon was for a time imprisoned in this château, to be freed only when Louis XI passed through the town and granted a general pardon to all criminals. I was happy to discover that this complex building, its various parts dating from the

Middle Ages to the eighteenth century, opens to visitors in summer.

So far after Orleans I had found no sign of St James of Compostela; but this failure was soon remedied. The Loire is bridged at Meung-sur-Loire, and five kilometres east of it is the tiny village of Cléry-Saint-André. On their way to Compostela pilgrims came here to pray before a statue of the Virgin Mary, discovered (it was said) in a thicket in 1280. It no longer succours pilgrims, for once again the Huguenots destroyed what they took to be a cause of superstitious heresy. Over the high altar today stands a sixteenth-century replica. That two French sovereigns, Louis XI (who died in 1483) and his second wife Charlotte of Savoy, lie interred here in the church of Notre-Dame is a testimony to the hold that miracle-working statues possessed over the medieval mind. Here too is enshrined the heart of King Charles VIII. Another testimony to the power of a miracle-working statue is the splendour of the huge fifteenth-century basilica which rises in the middle of this place and boasts a superb, flamboyant Gothic west window. The marauding English had destroyed an earlier church which housed the statue, and Louis XI himself ordered the present one to be rebuilt as a royal chapel in 1473, ten years before his death.

Though the statue is no more, the royal remains are still here. The custodian took me to the north aisle, pulled up a mouldering door let into the floor and revealed Louis XI's trepanned skull and the pinker skull of his second bride. The rest of their corpses are in a tomb with a statue of the kneeling monarch sculpted by Michel Bourdin in 1622 (a tomb which replaced one destroyed by the Huguenots). Having inspected their skulls I found my own way to the chapel of Saint-Jacques. In the early fifteenth century the canons of this church saw fit to commission two Brittany architects, the brothers Gilles and François de Pontbriand, to build this chapel, with its beautiful vaulting. A century later an unknown sculptor created for the chapel a spectacular statue of St James, a cockle shell in his hat, his beard and long hair curly and immaculately brushed. Pilgrims' staffs, girdles and purses are all incorporated in the lusciously carved vaults of this chapel, as well as (for a reason I cannot fathom) scourges.

I drove south-west and then turned right to cross the river again and reach Beaugency. The twenty-one arches of the eleventh-century bridge are ancient, irregular and gleam white above the blue waters. Until the eighteenth century this bridge carried a chapel dedicated to St James of Compostela, a sign that it was initially built to carry the press of pilgrims. Both the chapel and the fortifications of the town were demolished in 1767. The arches of the pilgrims' bridge are slightly out of line because of the Devil's anger. Convinced that no one in the eleventh century could have constructed such a long bridge, he insisted that it would tumble into the waters unless he could claim the soul of the first person to cross it. To foil him, as soon as the bridge was finished the mayor of Beaugency sent a cat across it, at which the enraged devil kicked part of its span off its original course.

Beaugency is where in 1152 King Louis VII and his wife Eleanor of Aquitaine managed to divorce each other – an event which was the origin of the Hundred Years' War and will influence this pilgrimage later on. Ostensibly their marriage was annulled because they were cousins. In truth, though he was a saint, she was so hot-blooded that they quarrelled even on a joint crusade against the Muslims. I suppose that St James of Compostela, in one of his later guises as Moor-slayer, would have approved of the crusade but not of the divorce. Pilgrims to his shrine were protected in this still partly fortified town by the Knights Templar, whose eleventh-century Romanesque hospice, with a sweetly decorated façade, I found in rue du Puits-de-l'Ange.

Good fortune still favoured me as I decided to turn west here and drive to Vendôme. By way of the sleepy villages of Josnes (whose neo-Romanesque church did not impress me) and Marchenoir (where I responded much more favourably to the fifteenth-century church of Notre-Dame), I reached another ancient pilgrimage centre, Saint-Léonard-en-Beauce. Léonard was a fifth-century hermit, a disciple of St Mesmin, who lived in the nearby Marchenoir forest and founded a chapel here. After his death he was buried inside it, and those who came to revere his bones found that they could work miracles. This accounts for the remarkable present-day church as Taint-Léonard-en-Beauce, which dates back as far as the twelfth century, boasts fine sculpted capitals and has a splendid belfry designed by a brilliant local architect, Jean Texier. Texier was known as Jean de Beauce and designed not only the new tower of Chartres cathedral but also the stupendous façade of Holy Trinity at Vendôme, for which I was making.

Perhaps the couple of glasses of wine I sipped sitting by the roadside just outside Saint-Léonard-en-Beauce were responsible for the fact that I mistakenly drove on not to Vendôme as I had planned but instead north-west to reach Fréteval. It was a happy error, for Fréteval is delightful, situated on the banks of the Loir and overlooked by the remains of a château built by the Counts of Blois in the late eleventh century and partly rased during the Hundred Years' War. Here in 1194 Richard Coeur de Lion defeated Philippe Auguste of France in battle. Fréteval has preserved its ancient tithe barn and some lovely Renaissance houses and manor-houses. A former priory abuts on to its church, which is dedicated to St Nicolas. Its seventeenth-century furnishings are quaint, with box pews and the pew numbers carved in each one on little bookstands. The splendid barrel-vault is braced by great wooden beams.

Just beyond the village I turned on to the N10 to reach Vendôme fourteen kilometres further on. On the way is the hamlet of Pezou, whose name derives from a Celtic word meaning 'humid'. Here the church of Saint-Pierre boasts a twelfth-century Romanesque porch. The enlightened parish priest has put some useful historical notes inside this church, and from them I learned that it was founded in 1079 as an appendage of the Abbey of Vendôme. Pezou church has the same hammerbeam roof as Saint-Nicolas, Fréteval, save that here the beams are yet more elaborate. The church also boasts an elegant eighteenth-century gallery. But for the parish priest's notes I should never have spotted that a painting of the deposition of the crucified Jesus was given to the church (as an inscription on its frame declares) by no less a personage than Napoleon Bonaparte, who passed through here in 1807.

Due south of Pezou at Lisle I discovered that the mid twelfth-century church is dedicated to Saint-Jacques. Much of it seems to have been rebuilt in the middle of the nineteenth century, but the porch remains authentically Romanesque. Then I reached Vendôme, crossed the Loir to turn into the town, and parked outside the church of La-Madeleine. La-Madeleine was founded in 1474 and boasts both a spiky Gothic spire and yet another of the barrel-vaulted, hammer-beam roofs typical of this region. Here angels as well as dragons are carved on the beams, the stained glass dates from the Renaissance, and the balcony bears a Gothic organ. St James instantly puts in an appearance, in the most important stained glass of the east window, where he is presenting the donor, Jacques Maslon, and his three sons to the Blessed Virgin Mary.

Immediately beyond the church square (the place de-la-Madeleine) the pilgrimage route appears in the guise of rue Saint-Jacques. It leads to the post office, immediately opposite which there rises the flamboyant Gothic belfry of the former pilgrimage chapel of Saint-Jacques. The chapel was built, initially in the twelfth century, by a fraternity who called themselves the *Fratres Condonati* and were dedicated to caring for sick or improverished pilgrims. Though officially styled 'brethren', they were joined by women who nursed pilgrims back to health.

Alongside the church, which was rebuilt in 1452, this charitable confraternity ran a hospice, which continued to welcome pilgrims till the eighteenth century. Today the church of Saint-Jacques serves as a state-owned art gallery, which displays the works of local artists and craftsmen. Once again the roof is barrel-vaulted, with fearsome beasts clutching the tie-beams. From the church I strolled along the pedestrianized and cobbled rue du Change, with its colourful awnings, shops and bars, to reach the glory of Vendôme, the church of the Holy Trinity.

As you cross a branch of the river here, a huge tree on the right bears a notice saying that it was planted in 1789, the year of the Revolution. Since the waters have washed away much of the soil around its roots, I do not think it will last much longer. Ahead, through the half-timbered houses, rises the ruined château of Vendôme. The ensemble of this town is superb. Gallo-Roman in origin, it was defended by this feudal château, which Geoffrey Martel enlarged in the eleventh century. He also founded the abbey of the Trinity in 1033. It housed one of the most fragile relics imaginable (one of Jesus's tears), which brought countless pilgrims and with them much wealth to Vendôme.

I had been to Vendôme before, but the sight of the church of the Holy Trinity which suddenly appears around a corner never fails to astound me. The flamboyant west façade shimmers like a stone fire. It was built between 1485 and 1509. Beside it, separate from the church, is the Romanesque belfry of 1129. The interior – simple and narrow – houses late fifteenth-century furnishings which include extremely sumptuous choir stalls. It is famous for housing the oldest stained glass depiction of the Madonna and the infant Jesus, dating from 1140. But by far the finest piece of stained glass in the whole abbey is that in a chapel to the right of the apse depicting St James of Compostela. A fifteenth-century glassmaker has portrayed the saint bootless, reading a book, a red robe thrown over his blue shift. On his bag and on his staff are cockle-shells.

France puts Britain to shame with its vast number of local bookshops, and (as at Etampes) at Vendôme I went into the one nearest to the abbey and asked for anything about the road to Santiago de Compostela. My reward was a locally-published work by Jean Bernadac entitled *Les Chemins de Saint Jacques en Vendômois*. Monsieur Bernadac has devilled about in the archives, producing nuggets which in part filled me with gloom, in part with joy. My gloom derived from the vast number of relics of the pilgrimage route that have disappeared. At Villers-sur-Loir, for instance, he asserts that in the twelfth-century church of Saint-Hilaire there was once a stained glass window depicting a pilgrim, his wife and their son, all sleeping in the same bed. Jean Bernadac has also discovered that at Trôo a church of Saint-Jacques once abutted on to a hospice also dedicated to the saint.

No trace of either remains. The most regrettable loss he recounts is
that of a medieval wall painting in the church of Saint-Pierre at Artins
which represented St James battling against the Moors. It seems to
have perished (M. Bernadac does not say how) in 1937.

Yet his book also brought me joy, and with him as my guide I
wandered through the countryside surrounding Vendôme searching
for traces of St James. Most of the sites mentioned by M. Bernadac lie
west of Vendôme. At Houssay I found a mid-nineteenth-century
church dedicated to the saint, inside which is his statue carved out of
stone. Close by is Lavardin guarded by a château half-demolished on
the orders of Henri IV at the end of the sixteenth century. Here a
Gothic bridge crosses the River Loir. The church is bleak and fortified, standing next to a tumbledown barn. The town is utterly entrancing. The wall paintings inside the church were in terrible condition when I saw them, but here is a memento of the pilgrimage to
Compostela. As you enter the nave you find a fifteenth-century
painting of St James. He is dressed as a pilgrim, sack in hand. At his
feet kneels another pilgrim, a pilgrim's staff across his shoulder.

Further west, by its very name Saint-Jacques-des-Guérets recalls
the saint of Compostela, and inside the church is a superb sequence of
late twelfth-century frescoes, one of which depicts the martyrdom of
St James. The bearded saint, carrying his book in his hand, turns his
head to the executioner, who – even as he wields the sword – is forgiven by his victim. In the nave St James appears again in a medieval
statue, his hat ornamented with a cockle-shell.

Then I drove back though some superb Loir valley villages and
towns – Montoire-sur-le-Loir the finest, Prunay-Cassereau the
second finest – to join the N10 just south of the hamlet of Villetou,
where a bas-relief in the church depicts St James with his staff and
bag. From here the tree-lined N10 took me into Tours. On the left,
just outside the city, I spotted the fortified manor-house and farm
which once belonged to the Maslon family, whose stained glass window dedicated to St James I had admired in the church of La-
Madeleine at Vendôme.

Tours is a strange city. The Second World War wreaked havoc
here. As a result a cluster of nasty modern buildings which replaced
those bombed during the conflict seems to hem in virtually every
ancient survival. This tedious pattern disappears only in the old
quarter, with place Plumereau enlivened by half-timbered houses
and surrounded by ancient streets with more half-timbered houses.
In the cathedral, dedicated to Saint-Gatien, you can trace the history
of Touraine architecture, from the thirteenth-century Gothic choir
by way of the flamboyant Gothic exterior to the Renaissance towers.

But on the way to Compostela pilgrims came to visit another great building. It scarcely exists today. This church rose above the tomb of St Martin, a native of Sabaria in upper Pannonia, born in the year 316. Serving as a distinguished Roman soldier, Martin became famous when he sliced his cloak in two to clothe a naked begger. Having become a monk, this former soldier had no desire to be consecrated a bishop. As the eighteenth-century hagiographer Alban Butler records, 'A stratagem was made use of to call him to the door of his monastery to give his blessing to a sick person, and he was forcibly conveyed to Tours under a strong guard. Some of the neighbouring bishops, who were called to assist at the election, urged that the meanness of his dress and appearance, and his slovenly air, showed him to be unfit for such a dignity. But such objections were commendations of the servant of God, who was installed in the episcopal chair.'

Alban Butler continued: 'Saint Martin in this new dignity continued the same manner of life, retaining the same humility of mind, austerity of life, and meanness of dress.' At first the new Bishop of Tours lived in a little cell beside his cathedral. So many people pressed upon him that he was eventually forced to retire outside the city, to live where now stand the ruins of the famous abbey of Marmoutier. From time to time he would emerge, working miracles, healing the sick, preaching to the heathen. When the time came for him to die, he insisted on lying down on ashes and hair-cloth, in spite of the entreaties of his disciples that a little straw might be put under his body. At first he was buried in the little oratory outside Tours where he died, but soon his followers brought his body to the city of which he had been bishop. And over his new grave rose a mighty abbey church.

To enthuse the pilgrims for Compostela to visit the basilica of St Martin at Tours, Aimery Picaud first waxed lyrical about the saint himself, 'the man who wondrously revived three dead men, made the lepers healthy, calmed the rowdy, and healed the sick, mad and demoniacs'. Aimery also described the superb reliquary in which the body of St Martin was enshrined, 'resplendent with a profusion of gold, silver and precious stones and decorated with scenes of many miracles.' As for the immense basilica which rose above it, this, according to Picaud, was modelled on the basilica of St James the Great at Compostela itself. 'The sick come here to pray and are healed,' the *Guide* continues, 'those possessed by demons are delivered from them, the blind see, the lame walk and every sort of sickness is healed. Whoever begs an act of grace here is granted total comfort.' The abbey church he knew was begun in the eleventh century, after pagan Normans had razed the basilica that had risen over the shrine of St Martin in the second half of the fifth century. The new church took two centuries to complete. The city that grew up around it now became a favourite resort of the French nobility, and King Louis XI made the Château de Plessis-lès-Tours his chief home. Tours also, incidentally, was where the Knights Templar, longtime protectors of pilgrims, were condemned in 1309 on charges of heresy and immorality.

The wars of religion brought disaster to the city and above all to the pilgrimage shrine. When the Huguenots took possession of the city in 1562 they held Tours for a mere ten days, but during that time, as they pillaged and sacked churches, managed to despoil St Martin's basilica. They also cremated the relics of the saint. Religious pride shifted elsewhere, in particular to the splendid cathedral of Saint-Gatien, and no one bothered to repair the basilica of St Martin. In 1802 the constructors of rue des Halles demolished the nave to make way for this new street. All that remains of the Romanesque basilica are a couple of towers, the clock-tower and the so-called tour Charlemagne (part of which fell down in 1928 and was rebuilt in what I regret was far from faithful to the original). As a result it is not easy to evoke the thrill which a medieval pilgrim must have felt at arriving in the city of the man who had evangelized France just as (they believed) St James had evangelized Spain. A gallery in the former convent courtyard (at number 3 in nearby rue Descartes) is all that remains of the former monastery of St Martin.

Eighty-five years after destroying the nave of St Martin's basilica, the city of Tours began making amends by building a new basilica in the Byzantine style. Building was prompted by the discovery of a rock-hewn tomb under the house which stood on the site of the high altar of the former basilica. The new church was finished in 1924, and its crypt stands where once stood the saint's exquisite shrine. I walked down the steps leading to where his body used to rest. The new tomb is impressive enough, but it is of course empty. Yet the absent Martin is evidently still working miracles, to judge from the modern ex-votos on the wall here thanking him for his help.

CHAPTER TWO

FROM VÉZELAY TO THE SEA

TOURS – MONTRICHARD – ROMORANTIN-LANTHENAY – AUBIGNY-SUR-
NÈRE – AUXERRE – VÉZELAY – LA CHARITÉ-SUR-LOIRE – BOURGES –
ISSOUDUN – LEVROUX – SAINTE-CATHERINE-DE-FIERBOIS – TAVANT –
CHÂTELLERAULT – POITIERS – PARTHENAY – SAINTES – PONS – BLAYS –
LIBOURNE – CASTILLON-LA-BATAILLE – LE SAUVE-MAJEUR – BORDEAUX.

A T TOURS I decided once again to desert Aimery Picaud's route from Orleans and take a trip east to Vézelay, partly because the spot is one of the great pilgrimage sites of western Christendom and partly because Picaud himself so much praises it. My route ran alongside the River Cher to the busy town of Montrichard, which is defended by a huge square keep and ancient walls. Foulques Nerra, Count of Anjou, built the keep in the early eleventh century, and in the next century the spot took the name 'Mons Trichardi' (the mount which carries the château of Trichardi). This apparent backwater of a town subsequently saw several key dynastic rituals of France. In 1476, for instance, the twelve-year-old Duke of Orleans (who became King Louis XII) was forced by his father to marry the daughter of Louis XI, Jeanne de France, who was three years younger than her husband. The Bishop of Orleans married them in the church of Sainte-Croix, which still stands here and was once the chapel of the château. Though this church is ancient, an even finer one, in my view, is the equally venerable church of Notre-Dame-de-Nanteuil. The hospice in rue porte-aux-Rois which once sheltered pilgrims was built over two centuries, half in the fifteenth, half in the sixteenth, and it still houses a charming Renaissance chapel. Yet quainter is the sixteenth-century house built on the bridge to control the river traffic.

The villages along this route are stunningly beautiful. At Saint-Aignan men and boys were fishing in the River Cher. I spent half an hour in the remarkable twelfth-century church, with its crypt and astonishing set of carved capitals, before walking up to the Renaissance château where no one stopped me wandering into its courtyard. Then I drove on to Selles-sur-Cher, where in the sixth century a hermit built himself a cell which gave the picturesque town its name.

This part of France seems to me at times to consist entirely of river-side villages with magical churches defended by equally magical châteaux. Selles-sur-Cher is no exception, with the additional delight that no fewer than three rivers keep it cool (the Fouzon and the Sauldre as well as the Cher) and in addition it is traversed by the Canel du Berry.

My next staging-post on the way to Vézelay, Romorantin-Lanthenay, lies on the River Sauldre and is dominated by a château rebuilt by Jean of Angoulême between 1448 and 1467. No fewer than three churches were begun here in the twelfth century. In one of them, the deconsecrated Saint-Pierre-de-Monthault, I found a seventeenth-century statue of St Roch, a favourite saint of pilgrims to Compostela. He is here because amongst his many gifts is the ability to protect people from the plague, a service which he had performed for the citizens of Romorantin-Lanthenay in 1584 and 1595.

By now I was beginning to regret my desire to visit Vézelay, for the journey there, though delightful enough, seemed to be becoming endless. So I stayed the night at Salbris. The next morning nothing looked impossible, and my spirits perked up as I passed through Souesmes, with its châteaux and half-timbered houses. Aubigny-sur-Nère was still more entrancing, for this was a town taken up by the Stuarts long before thier exile from Britain in the seventeenth century. One of them, so the local guide-book relates, was named John and in the fifteenth century brought a large contingent of Scottish troops to assist the French in the wars against the English. Aubigny-sur-Nère has adopted his coat of arms: three golden buckles. A devout man as well as a warrior, he made a pilgrimage to the Holy Land, before finally losing his life at the battle of Harengs, close by Orleans, in 1428.

By way of two beautiful towns, Saint-Fargeau with its Renaissance château and Toucy which boasts narrow twisting streets and half-timbered houses, I drove to Auxerre before finally winding my way down south to Vézelay. My reason for visiting Auxerre was an unforgettable experience from the time when my children were young. Sitting high on the hill which dominates this ensemble of superb sanctuaries, we were picnicking when my younger daughter – then aged three or so – simply walked to the edge and fell twenty feet down amongst the thistles and thorns. Naturally I shot down after her, and both of us for a day or so suffered miserably from nettle rash and prickles.

There are better reasons for visiting Auxerre: a splendid ensemble of houses in its old quarter, dating from the fifteenth to the eighteenth centuries; the thirteenth century stained glass of its flamboyant-

Gothic cathedral, which rises from a Romanesque crypt; and the fourteenth century Gothic belfry of the abbey of Saint-Germain, in whose crypt are mid-ninth century wall-paintings – amongst the oldest in France. At Saint-Bris-le-Vineux a few kilometres south-east a twelfth century hostel of the Knights Templars reminds us of the protectors of medieval pilgrims to Santiago de Compostela.

Finally I reached the hamlet of Asquins just north of Vézelay and was back on the pilgrims' road to Compostela. Situated by the River Cure on what was once a Roman road, Asquins, in all probability, is where Aimery Picaud lived btween 1135 and 1140 when he was writing his *Liber sancti Jacobi*, so fittingly the church is dedicated to Saint Jacques and inside it is a reliquary bust of the saint. Three kilometres further south I reached the still-fortified village of Vézelay.

Here, wrote Aimery Picaud, above all the pilgrim must venerate the sacred bones of St Mary Magdalene. 'She is in truth the glorious Mary who, in the house of Simon the Leper, washed the feet of Jesus with her tears, dried them with her hair and anointed them with a costly perfume while kissing them,' he continued; 'and for this reason her many sins were forgiven, because she greatly loved the one who loves all humankind, Jesus Christ, her Saviour.' Picaud went on to recount the legend of her arrival in Provence, in the company of St Maximin and other disciples of Jesus. Maximin had buried Mary Magdalene at Aix-en-Provence, and there she lay until a monk of Vézelay named Badilon arrived at the city. Although Picaud does not say so, at that moment Aix-en-Provence was smitten by the plague. In return for food an old man led Badilon to the relics of the saint, recognizable by their fragrant odour.

This was an era of grave-robbing, especially when the grave contained such venerable bones. Badilon even alleged that the same evening the Magdalene appeared to him in a dream, begging to have her relics transported to Vézelay. Aimery Picaud takes up the tale by recounting that after their arrival 'a great and beautiful basilica was built for her, and an abbey of monks was founded there. For love of the saint, sins were forgiven; the blind received their sight; the mouths of the dumb were unstopped; the lame began to walk; the possessed were delivered; and inexpressible benefits were accorded to many believers.'

The cult and prosperity of Vézelay did not last long. The rumour that the monastery had acquired the bones of the saint began circulating only in the mid-eleventh century. To the alarm of the monks, in 1280 the Provençals claimed that they still possessed the relics of St Mary Magdalene, and the final blow came a few years later when Pope Boniface VIII declared that he too believed her bones resided elsewhere. But for a time this was a principle shrine for any pilgrim. Archbishop Thomas Becket, driven from England by Henry II, sought refuge at Vézelay. From here in 1190 Richard Coeur de Lion set off with King Philippe-August of France on their fateful voyage to the Holy Land. The miniscule hill-village prospered, its Romanesque houses welcomed pilgrims as did the former hospice which is still here, and its monks created the superb monastery, much of which remains to this day. Abbot Arthaud began building it in 1104, but the Romanesque church he inaugurated was soon replaced with a splendid, half-Romanesque, half-Gothic building under the rule of Abbots Renaud de Semur (1106-1128) and Albéric (1128-1138). Work ended under the rule of Abbot Ponce de Montboissier (1138-1161).

The monastery at Vézelay suffered over subsequent centuries. During the wars of religion the town passed into the hands of the Protestants, who are said to have turned part of the monastery into a pigsty and stables. The whole monastic community was suppressed at the time of the Revolution. In the nineteenth century the ubiquitous Gothic restorer Viollet-le-Duc came to the rescue of the decayed façade of the abbey church, which makes one unsure whether or not what can be seen is authentically medieval.

Yet I remain impressed, and even more so by the carvings over the central door of the narthex, a sort of vestibule where pilgrims could gather in anticipation of visiting the Magdalene's shrine. The robes of the Christ in Majesty reveal his gaunt limbs beneath them. His face is stern, his beard neatly combed. Bizarre figures accompany the well-known ones, and one man climbs on to his horse by means of a ladder. A dog curls its legs around its neck, and an acrobat attempts to do likewise, while next to them a mermaid broods alone. The signs of the zodiac and the labours of the months are sculpted here. I like very much the symbol of the dying year in a roundel on the right-hand side of this porch: a man carrying an old woman on his shoulders.

The left doorway has a tympanum carved with scenes after the resurrection of Jesus, while the right one illustrates his infancy. The carved capitals are no less entrancing – and there are altogether 123 of them. To single out a few of them is perhaps foolish, but my favourites include a scene of St Benedict raising a child from the dead. The dead baby lies completely wrapped up in swaddling clothes, while its father lays a hand against his cheek in despair. Another superb capital depicts David cutting off the head of the giant Goliath, who is wearing medieval chain-mail.

The nave remains Romanesque, tall and cool, reaching into an early Gothic thirteenth-century choir and flanked by Gothic transepts. Vézelay abbey has also preserved its chapter house, and in the crypt is a modern reliquary inside which are bones which may or may not be those of St Mary Magdalene.

At Vézelay I searched and searched but could find no capital depicting St James the Great. Apart from St Mary Magdalene and St Benedict, the other local saint depicted here is St Martin of Tours smashing down a tree idolatrously worshipped by the pagans of this land. (Some of the heathen are vainly trying to hold it up with ropes.) I did not encounter St James again until I had driven further south-west to La Charité-sur-Loire, where the Cluniacs founded a cele-brated monastery in 1059. His statue is inside the church of Sainte-Croix. The magnificent city of Bourges, as I had expected, also offers evidence of the survival of the cult of St James of Compostela from the thirteenth into the fifteenth century, not simply because the saint is depicted in the superb glass of the choir chapels in the cathedral, but also because at a time when Bourges was the capital of France its most famous and richest citizen, the merchant and banker Jacques Coeur, incorporated the saint's cockle-shells into his own armorial device.

Jacques Coeur was born in this cathedral city towards the end of the fourteenth century. The son of a furrier, his financial cunning and political skills, the wealth he gained from trading in wool, wheat, spices and silk, and his acumen in lending money to King Charles VII who needed to pay an army that was recovering Normandy from the English, all combined to make him one of the most powerful men in France. Through his influence his brother became Bishop of Luçon. His son Jean was consecrated Archbishop of Bourges. And Jacques himself built the finest private home in France. The Palais de Jacques-Coeur at Bourges incorporates two of the ancient Roman towers which once defended the city; but it is chiefly a beautifully decorated early Renaissance palace. It was finished in 1443, and the principal motif of its embellishments is the coat of arms of its owner, bearing three hearts and three cockle-shells.

Though Bourges cathedral is dedicated to St Stephen, its monu-ments and stained glass windows continually glorify the pilgrim saint of Compostela. The chapel of St Ursin, who was first Bishop of Bourges, has a window depicting St James. In the crypt he appears in a sculpted entombment of Jesus, dressed as a pilgrim, with staff and cockle-shell. Thanks to the bounty of four cathedral canons, he appears again in a window in the chapel of St Anne.

The stained glass of the chapel of St François de Sales is entirely devoted to the legend of St James. In the first medallion the magician Hermogenus sends an envoy named Philetus to dissuade James from the Christian faith. Instead James converts Philetus. Enraged, Hermogenus casts a spell over Philetus which paralyses him, but James's cloak warms his stiff limbs and he is healed. Next Hermogenus sends a posse of devils to capture Philetus, who is now James's loyal aide. St James responds by turning the devils on Hermogenus himself. Hermogenus, now in thrall to a demon, is rescued by the intervention of James and in gratitude becomes a Christian and burns most of his magic books, throwing the others into the sea. Pleasingly, he preaches the gospel armed with one of James's walking sticks. The rest of the stained glass concludes with the trial and martyrdom of St James, during which he manages to heal a paralytic and convert one of his prosecutors named Josias, who himself gladly embraces martyrdom.

I drove south-west from Bourges along the N151 to Issoudun on the River Théols, where I followed the signs for the Musée, expecting some dry-as-dust local history museum, and found instead a treasure. The signs took me south of Issoudun, around its fortified wall and through a medieval gateway to reach the former pilgrims' hospice and hospital of the town. It is dedicated to St Roch and was founded by the canons of the collegiate church of Saint-Cyr in 1144. Today's buildings date from the fifteenth to the eighteenth centuries. To care for the sick the monks planted medicinal herbs in their garden, which is still cultivated and still overlooked by their quarters and balcony. In 1646 a pharmacy was added to the hospice's resources. The monks appointed an apothecary, whose emoluments included free food and lodgings. Preserved today are the seventeenth- and eighteenth-century enamel jars, labelled with the different drugs and medicines they once contained and stacked in purpose-built cupboards around the walls. Some of the ingredients of the medicines (crayfish eyes, dragon's blood) might still be effective. Here too are tables bearing primitive surgical instruments, as well as a copper still used for distilling remedies that needed an alcoholic base.

The chapel is beautiful, constructed around 1500. Sick men and women were segregated in this hospital, but they could come together at the time of Mass, allowed to watch it only through a shuttered window and to receive Holy Communion through a hole in the wall, so as not to infect (it was hoped) the healthy. Inside the chapel are two superbly carved Jesse trees. They depict the ancestors of Jesus, his supposedly royal as well as his religious forebears. But at the heart of one of them in his pilgrim's hat perches not one of these but St James of Compostela.

This chapel houses another sculpted head of St James, as well as several ancient pilgrims' staffs. The collegiate church of Saint-Cyr also possesses a chapel dedicated to the saint. And from here I drove south, turning right along the D8 just outside the town to find at the little town of Levroux even more remarkable historical testimonies to the pilgrims who walked to Compostela.

Levroux took its name from a leper (or *lépreux*) reputedly healed here by St Martin of Tours. But it is St James of Compostela whose memory haunts the town today. I walked through the fortified town gate which dates from the late fifteenth century and discovered a house of the same date known as the *Maison de Jacques*, because once pilgrims would spend a night there. Further on along rue Victor-Hugo rises the church of Saint-Sylvain, its west porch sculpted in the thirteenth century with figures opening their own coffin lids and rising from death to await the Last Judgement. Among the many treasures inside the soaring nave of the church is a fifteenth-century statue of St James the pilgrim, a cockle-shell on his hat.

I wound west back to the N10 by way of Sainte-Catherine-de-Fierbois, a remarkably sweet, quiet village, especially considering its proximity to the juggernauts charging along the N10. The plethora of saints connected with this hamlet is remarkable. Here St James is but one of three revered figures of Christendom. The name of the spot derives from St Catherine of Alexandria, who was broken on a wheel for refusing to marry a Roman emperor and then beheaded. In the early fifteenth century a local notable, the Maréchal de Boucicaut, brought back a fragment of her bones from Mount Sinai, where today most of her corpse is enthroned in the sanctuary of a Greek Orthodox monastery. So many pilgrims *en route* to Compostela varied their journey to venerate this relic that in 1415 the Maréchal de Boucicaut was obliged to build a hospice and almonry for them at Sainte-Catherine-de-Fierbois, a building which today serves as the town hall and presbytery of this tiny place. The church nearby is a lovely Gothic building with a superb flamboyant porch, and inside is a fifteenth-century statue of St Catherine. She holds the sword which decapitated her, and stands on a wheel which broke rather than crushing her to death. Another reminiscence of St James, the Moor-slayer, persisted here. Legend alleged that Charles Martel, having repulsed the Saracens, left his sword behind the high altar of the church. On 15 March 1429, Joan of Arc stayed at Sainte-Catherine-de-Fierbois and prayed before the statue of the saint of Alexandria. The saintly statue apparently told her that the fabulous sword was still there. Instead of taking it instantly, Joan of Arc left the village, sending back an emissary three days later who did find the sword and brought it to his leader.

Tavant was my next stop, an even tinier monastic village to be found a dozen and a half kilometres south-west just beyond a spot known as l'Ile-Bouchard. A sheet of paper pinned to the door of the locked Romanesque church of Saint-Nicolas gave the address of the lady who keeps the key. She took a little money off me and expounded first of all the capitals of the church, relishing a wild beast eating a sad, naked man. Then she showed me the frescoes of the crypt. The most famous, as she rightly observed, depicts the sin of lust, in the form of a beautiful woman, blood dripping from her breast, which has been pierced with a lance. Blue and yellow, red, green, black and white, some of the pictures merely sketched out without any colouring, these frescoes are as moving as any I know. Here St Peter is crucified, upside down as tradition has it, for he deemed himself unworthy to be executed in the same fashion as his Lord. King David strums a harp. Men are depicted building the Temple of Jerusalem. Jesus harrows hell. Every gesture reveals the influence of Byzantium. But what interested me most of all was a twelfth-century (or maybe even eleventh-century) painting of a pilgrim on the right of the entrance. Wearing sandals and a hat with a turned-up brim, carrying a palm branch, a bag for his food and a staff, he is clearly off to Compostela, though he does not wear the cockleshell badge of St James. Why the palm branch? I have read that the habit had grown up of planting palm branches at Roncesvalles in the Pyrenees, as pilgrims passed by a cross reputedly placed there by Charlemagne. It seems an unlikely theory, for the branch carried by this pilgrim would undoubtedly be dead by the time he reached Roncesvalles from Tavant.

By now I was back on the main pilgrimage route from Paris. On the way to Compostela pilgrims received hospitality at the monastery of Notre-Dame in Tavant. Today it lies in ruins. Regaining the N10 I drove south to Châtellerault. In spite of its exceptionally boring outskirts, the heart of the town is stunning. In the tree-shaded main square stands a newly-cleaned flamboyant church dedicated to St John the Baptist. On the day I arrived its peace was shattered by a raucous fair filling the square. Imprudently I took a ride on the ghost train. The puny ghosts failed to unsettle me, but the speed of the ride did, and I sped into the nearest bar to ask the proprietress if there were *toilettes* available. 'Only for customers,' was her prim reply, so I had to control my nausea enough to order a thin beer.

Founded in the tenth century (according to an informative placard outside the church of Saint-Jean-Baptiste), Châtellerault had the status of a city by the seventeenth century. In the thirteenth Hospitallers built here a commandery whose chapel still stands. Châtellerault became rich partly by taxing those who wanted to use its ancient bridge to cross over the River Vienne and partly by trading in furs, armour and cutlery. The useful map on the placard guided me along boulevard Moissac and then south through a pedestrianized quarter with some lovely sixteenth- and seventeenth-century houses as far as rue Saint-Jacques, at the top of which stands the church of Saint-Jacques. Built in the eleventh century and much restored in the nineteenth, it has retained on its west façade a magnificent frieze, which depicts the enthroned Christ flanked by his twelve apostles. Over the doorway James the Great appears again, carved out of wood. The interior of the building is cool, almost all in the Romanesque style save for some twelfth-century Angevin Gothic vaulting. It shelters a marvellous baroque statue of St James the Great, sculpted in the seventeenth century. On his hat are no fewer than five cockleshells, with another seven on his mantle. Equipped for the journey as he is with staff and breadbasket, I should have thought it better were he wearing boots rather than sandals.

From the east end of the church I walked down rue Sully, passing on the left the Hôtel Sully, on which a notice informs you that the man who built it in 1600, Charles Androuet du Cerceau, also had a hand in rebuilding the ancient bridge. Châtellerault became a Protestant town during the wars of religion, and the Protestant leader, Henri IV of France, made it one of his headquarters. The magical bridge, with its seven irregular arches and a couple of defensive towers, fittingly bears the king's name and stretches across the Vienne at the end of rue Sully. The river here is wide, and it was also low when I visited Châtellerault, so that in mid-stream appeared islands with trees growing on them. One of the locals told me it was unusually low for the month, which was early February. He was watching his dog, which obviously loved running in and out of the river. It will swim no more, for before our eyes the little animal disappeared beneath the waters, its distraught master unable to help and claiming that his pet had been pulled under by a rat.

Medieval pilgrims and I now followed the route of the N10 from Châtellerault towards Poitiers. On the way they would have paused at La Tricherie, where you can still see the ruins of the almonry that gave them shelter as well as the well-preserved Romanesque monastery church. Poitiers itself was for these Christians of enormous historical importance, since here in 732 Charles Martel had inflicted such a military blow on the Saracens as to end their invasions of northern France. Spiritually it represented for them the birthplace of St Hilary the Great, who became its first bishop and was the man who ordained St Martin of Tours. Hilary was great both as a theologian and a miracle worker. (In 1851 the Catholic church decreed that he was one of the official Fathers of the church.) If Aimery Picaud is to be believed, theological opponents needed to fear his miraculous powers quite as much as his intellectual superiority. Aimery records that at one council when the saint was combatting the heresy of Arianism, one of the heretics retired to the latrines where he virtually exploded to death.

As at Tours, the architectural delights of Poitiers are by no means entirely connected with the respective patron saints of the cities. The church of Notre-Dame-la-Grande is often claimed to be the greatest Romanesque building in France, and its twelfth-century sculpted façade alone might justify that claim. Next to it rise the present-day law courts of the city, incorporating part of the medieval palace of the Counts of Poitou. I took rue de la Cathédrale south-east from here to the cathedral of Saint-Pierre. By contrast with the Romanesque of Notre-Dame-la-Grande, the cathedral, though begun in 1162, is today almost entirely Gothic in style. Before finding the church housing the remains of St Hilary, I went inside to stand before the marvellous twelfth- and thirteenth-century stained glass, and to admire the thirteenth-century stalls which are among the oldest surviving in France. Behind the cathedral is the eleventh-century church of Sainte-Radegone, a reminder that along with St Hilary this sixth-century French queen is joint patron saint of Poitiers. She died in 587, and her bones still lie in the crypt.

I found my way to the church of Saint-Hilaire-le-Grand by way of a building remarkable chiefly for its antiquity. The massive square baptistry of Saint-Jean, which stands near the city's archaeological and fine art museums, dates in part form the fourth century, and thus constitutes France's oldest religious building. St Hilary's own church stands further south-west. The bulk of it was built in the first half of the twelfth century. Unfortunately a bell-tower collapsed in 1590, ruining in part the nave and the six aisles. What we see today of these aisles is a nineteenth-century restoration. Yet the church remains impressive; its nave is topped with octagonal cupolas; the huge apse comprises a deambulatory – a sure sign of a church once besieged by pilgrims, who would be shepherded around the radiating chapels – and in the crypt is the authentic body of St Hilary himself.

From Poitiers I drove west for fifty-one kilometres to the fortified town of Parthenay, which is rich in memories of the pilgrimage route to Compostela. To the north of the town the fortifications of Parthenay incorporate a monumental machicolated gateway, which is still known as the Porte Saint-Jacques. Beside it rise three towers of the former citadel, both gate and citadel dating from the thirteenth century. Porte Saint-Jacques leads into the picturesque rue de la Vaux-Saint-Jacques, which is lined by half-timbered houses built in the fifteenth and sixteenth centuries. Though not one of the greatest of the churches of Parthenay, that dedicated to Saint-Jacques is a spirited piece of fifteenth-century architecture. And three kilometres south-west, on the edge of the town, is the suburb of Parthenay-le-Vieux, whose Cluniac monastery was once the home of Aimery Picaud himself. The quaint Romanesque church which served Aimery and his monastery still stands, the façade sumptuously sculpted.

It was time to drive south again, by way of Niort to Fénioux, which lies in the undulating countryside close by Saint-Jean-d'Angély. Saint-Jean-d'Angély once welcomed pilgrims into an abbey and its church which claimed to possess the head of St John the Baptist. In 1621 Protestants razed it to the ground – along with much else here, so that the town had to be mostly rebuilt and in consequence bears a charming Renaissance and classical look. The ruins of the abbbey, which was founded in 817, stand as a spectacular monument to religious bigotry. Little Fénioux escaped such ravages, and apart from its rebuilt belfry the rest of the parish church there remains Romanesque. It boasts a particularly successful sculpted doorway. But what above all drew me here was my desire to see one of the first examples of the influence of Muslim architecture on the road to Santiago. In the graveyard is a strange tower, created from eight columns, which resembles a Seleucid minaret.

By the N150 I continued south to the fine town and renowned pilgrimage centre of Saintes. Aimery Picaud tells the improving tale of St Eutropius, its first bishop, who preached the gospel here in the third century. According to Picaud, Persian blood flowed in the veins of Eutropius, for his father was an Emir of Babylon named Xerxes and his mother a Persian queen named Guiva. Picaud's tale is scarcely credible, since he places Eutropius's birth two centuries too early and even has him take part in the feast when Jesus miraculously multiplied loaves and fishes to feed a huge crowd. He does however include in his narrative St Eustella, daughter of the Roman governor of Saintes, who was converted by Eutropius and preferred to leave her rich home and live close by the saint's cell. Her enraged father commanded the butchers of Saintes to kill Eutropius, and Eustella found him dead in his cell one morning, a meat-cleaver through his skull.

Eustella buried the saint, and was herself later martyred in the Roman amphitheatre at Saintes. A fountain dedicated to her rises at the place where she died. Her corpse was interred close by that of Eutropius. In 1081 the Cluniacs, promotors of the pilgrimage road to Compostela, began raising a massive church over their bones, which the French Pope Urban II himself consecrated in 1096. The relics of Eutropius and Eustella still lie here in the Romanesque crypt. His slab is inscribed simply Eutropius. Having venerated these ancient bones, pilgrims would find shelter for the night in the guest room of the abbbey of Sainte-Marie-aux-Dames, which the Count of Anjou had founded in 1047. The harmonious abbey buildings which survive had been rebuilt in the eighteenth century, though the twelfth-century church was untouched. Napoleon Bonaparte transformed them into a barracks. Happily, the religious returned in 1938, and Sainte-Marie-aux-Dames is a monastery again.

I was heading for the coast, ignoring the motorway and taking instead the N137 to Blaye. On the way, at Pons, I came upon a far humbler and in some respects more telling testimony to the pilgrims of the Middle Ages. Pons is beautifully situated on a fortified site above the River Seugne. As well as boasting a Renaissance château, the town is dominated by its square Romanesque keep, which dates from 1185. The most evocative building is undoubtedly the hospice built in the twelfth and thirteenth centuries to shelter pilgrims to Compostela. It stands in the lower part of the town, close by the eleventh-century church of Saint-Vivien. On their way to Bordeaux pilgrims passed out of the hospice through the twelfth-century Porte Saint-Gilles. Pausing there some of them have carved horseshoes and others crosses – medieval graffiti testifying to their means of transport and their faith.

Forty-one kilometres further south I reached Blaye. The town is situated just beyond the spot where the rivers Dordogne and Garonne meet to form the mighty estuary which is known as La Gironde. Blaye overlooks the estuary itself. Since the locals here have the pleasing habit of calling the two rivers 'seas', the wine-growing region between them has come to be called *l'Entre-Deux-Mers*. As for the waters of the Garonne, they flow from our destination, Spain herself. Such a confluence could not fail to attract the Romans, who in 26 BC established here a camp which, after their retreat from the region, was replaced by a Merovingian fortress. After this fortress had been demolished by Guillaume d'Aquitaine, the Comte de Blaye built another in the early twelfth century.

With such a history you naturally expect a powerfully defended town, and are not disappointed. Remnants of the medieval fortress still remain, but the most impressive part of Blaye today is the mighty fortress finished here in 1688 by Vauban, Louis XIV's military architect and engineer. I am a fan of Vauban's, whose citadels proliferate throughout France, from the channel coast to the Pyrenees, and I marvel how this genius managed to get around to oversee them all. I also remain impressed at his skill in creating within them remarkably civilized mini-towns, their monuments frequently lauding his royal patrons. That at Blaye is no exception. If you want to drive inside you use the porte Royale, whereas on foot you use the porte Dauphine. Inside, what fascinated me was to discover the cloister of a convent, having not seen such preserved anywhere else in Vauban's fortresses (but then, I have not yet seen them all).

Pilgrims to Compostela came to see a different treasure at Blaye: the crypt of the church of Saint-Romain, in which (so the *Chanson de Roland* asserted) Charlemagne had laid the bodies of Roland and Oliver, as well as some others amongst his knights who had been slain on the Roncesvalles pass. Certainly some corpses lay here by the twelfth century and were dubbed those of these heroes. In the sixteenth century King François I made a pilgrimage to Blaye, had the tombs opened and peered at the dusty remains. These relics had long eclipsed the fame of the saint to whom the church is dedicated. Romain evangelized this region in the fifth century. Over his tomb this celebrated medieval church had risen. The building is today a ruin – I regret to say partly Vauban's fault, for he found it a troublesome interference with his own plans and demolished most of it – but its crypt can still be found. I do not think that the corpses of Roland and Oliver truly ever lay here, for this part of their story is legend and not history. Yet because they died fighting the Moors, the cult of Compostela soon included them in its pantheon of saints. The tomb which (it was claimed) held their venerated corpses was unfortunately destroyed by the English during the Hundred Years' War.

Some pilgrims to Compostela would next take ship from here to Bordeaux, but the evidence I discovered by not doing so reveals that many of them must have found other ways. This route also enables one to explore remarkable testimonies to the perils of the Hundred Years' War, namely a remarkable series of those fortified medieval cities known as *bastides*. From Blaye south-east to the town of Bourg (where you reach the River Dordogne) I followed a spectacular route along the so-called *Corniche Girondine*. Bourg itself is dominated by an impressive eighteenth-century château. Continuing from here along the short road that curves upstream to Saint-André-de-Cubzac I counted no fewer than three villages (Prignac, Saint-Gervais and Saint-Laurent-d'Arce) all still boasting Romanesque churches. Then among the vineyards appears the splendid and elegant Château du Bouilh, a totally different affair designed in the late eighteenth century by the exuberant architect Victor Louis (who is today more famous for the Grand Théatre of Bordeaux).

At Saint-André-de-Cubzac once stood a priory whose Romanesque church still survives. In the fifteenth century, like many in this region, it was fortified as a precaution against hostilities – evidence of the danger faced by the medieval pilgrims. This section of their route is one of the many much fought over by the English and the French, ever since Eleanor of Aquitaine – to the rage of the French – brought it to the English as part of her dowry, on her marriage to Henry II Plantagenet in 1152.

Throughout these perilous times the supply of pilgrims never died out, and from Saint-André-de-Cubzac I took the virtually straight road (until the River Dordogne forces it to veer) which they too would have followed as far as Libourne. At Fronsac, just outside this town, I climbed up for a magical panorama over the river.

In those troubled times the pilgrims were fortunate to find new places of refuge. In an attempt to ensure that their subjects would remain loyal to whoever was momentarily winning superiority in the long wars, both the English and French monarchs were founding fortified *bastides*. Their intention was to attract a special kind of citizen – sometimes from far afield – into the *bastide's* protective walls. The inhabitants of these new towns were afforded far more rights than most ordinary feudal underlings. They were given fertile territory to farm (hence these *bastides* are usually still surrounded by prosperous lands). Few *bastides* boast a feudal château, for this would have repelled the free-spirited supporters the rival monarchs hoped to attract. All of them possessed defensive gateways and walls, and – insofar as the lie of the land allowed it – were laid out in a grid pattern so that the citizens when defending themselves from attack could speed more easily from one threatened rampart to another.

Libourne is the first such town on this route to Compostela. Its name derives from the English seneschal Roger of Leyburn, who founded it at the strategic confluence of the Dordogne and the Isle in 1268. Here is the grid pattern of all these towns, and an arcaded market place. I wish the rue Gambetta did not cruelly cut through its old streets, yet this cannot destroy its charm, or that of its sixteenth-century town hall which stands in a square of equally delightful houses, most of the same date.

Napoleon I had a bridge built across the river here, but instead of crossing over I wanted to drive on to Castillon-la-Bataille. Here the Hundred Years' War finally ended in 1453 after a siege by the French King Charles VII. The seventy-five-year-old John Talbot, Earl of Shrewsbury and Watford, marched from Bordeaux in an attempt to lift the siege. In a disastrous error, he decided that his troops should fight with their backs to the river, making retreat impossible. When Talbot's horse was brought down, trapping the earl beneath it, a French archer killed him with an axe. As the rest of his army tried to flee, many of the soldiers were also slaughtered. A few months later

Charles VII was master of all of Gascony and Guyenne (a name which derives from the English deformation of Aquitaine). After the battle of Castillon the town proudly added the words 'la-Bataille' to its name.

One of my daughters lives not far from here, so I went to eat and stay a night with her. Then, to follow the pilgrim route and to find still more architectural legacies of the struggles which had ravaged this exquisite land, I drove the winding route south from Castillon-la-Bataille through Blasimon to Sauveterre-de-Guyenne. Both Blasimon and Sauveterre-de-Guyenne are *bastides*. The prosperity such *bastides* eventually brought to the region is evinced by the ancient windmills as well as the vineyards surrounding Blasimon. A further example of the prosperity that produced fine buildings is offered by the remains of the Benedictine abbey church of Blasimon, whose façade was richly sculpted both in the twelfth and the late sixteenth century – a reminder too of the pilgrims to Compostela who would have sought shelter with the monks.

In between these two *bastides*, at the hamlet of Puch, I came across another remnant of their medieval protectors, the Romanesque church of the Knights Templar. I have failed to discover exactly when Blasimon was transformed into a *bastide*, or by whom, but the history of Sauveterre-de-Guyenne is better documented. Edward I of England founded it in 1281. His aim in doing so was not rewarded, for Sauveterre-de-Guyenne changed hands back and forth from English to French throughout his reign and afterwards. It remains magical, its four Gothic gates still surviving, as well as its market place.

Then the great abbey at La Sauve-Majeure, some thirty kilometres north-west on the way to Bordeaux, bears remarkable testimony to the fact that the pilgrims of St James passed by. La Sauve-Majeure derives its name from the Latin *silva major* (though in truth most of the forests have here disappeared). What dominate the tiny village are the remains of a great abbey founded here in 1079 by St Gérard, whose own mortal remains lie in the parish church of Saint-Pierre. St James himself is sculpted both on a Romanesque capital of the ruined abbey (which was abandoned by the monks after the French Revolution) and also inside the parish church. What is more, one of the sixteenth-century frescoes behind the apse of Saint-Pierre also depicts the saint presenting a Christian with a pilgrim's staff. Another depicts a Compostela pilgrim praying to the Virgin Mary.

Three kilometres further on towards Bordeaux, driving through these medieval battlefields, I came upon another former *bastide*, namely Créon. As for Bordeaux itself, in spite of the horrors of the

Hundred Years' War the city greatly profited from the English connection, for her wines were welcome by the British. Under French
rule her trade disastrously declined. Next the whole region had to en-
dure both the wars of religion and the depradations of the peasants
who revolted in the mix-seventeenth century. And at the French
Rovolution Bordeaux cathedral – though still well worth visiting –
was deconsecrated and turned into a warehouse.

Although some treasures of older eras remain (and I particularly
relish the splendid Gothic church of Saint-Michel, with its fifteenth-
century masterpiece of a belfry), Bordeaux's architectural heyday
was the eighteenth century, for then prosperity returned. A quarter
beside the river preserves in its paved, narrow streets on the pattern
laid out in the Middle Ages, but the ancient ramparts were demolished as the city expanded. In the first half of the century Jacques
Gabriel and his son Jacques-Ange Gabriel created the beautiful place
de la Bourse, though the elegant Bourse itself is perhaps slightly too
monumental. It pales in grandeur beside the Corinthian columns of
the Grand Théatre, which Victor Louis built in the seven years before
1780 on the site of the former Roman forum. Ten years earlier had
risen the classically restrained but still huge Palais-Rohan, which is
now the town hall.

Bordeaux thus seems an unlikely spot to retain traces of medieval
pilgrims. The truth is quite other. Since I find it a delightful city, its
airport my speediest way into my favourite part of France, I had
frequently toured its streets and visited its churches before making
this pilgrimage to Compostela. To seek out the evidences of former
pilgrims was a particular pleasure.

Two appeared almost immediately, just over the Pont-de-Pierre
in the fourteenth-century church of Saint-Michel. The first is a chapel
dedicated to St James, and evidently built in the epoch before this
church was Gothicized, for although its altar dates from 1622, it incorporates work of the early eleventh century. The second is a paint
ing of 1631 depicting the apotheosis of the saint. Spanish in origin, it
must have been brought here by a seventeenth-century pilgrim on his
way home, along with the Spanish statue it houses.

Rue des Faures and then elegant cours Victor-Hugo lead from
this church to what has become the chief symbol of Bordeaux, the
great fifteenth-century gate and belfry which is today known as the
tour de la Grosse Cloche. Its connection with Compostela seems
initially remote, but the clue lies in the name of the street into which it
leads – not rue Saint-Jacques but rue Saint-James, spelled in the
English way and a legacy of the ancient connection. (This same spell-
ing I have spotted at Bergerac, nearby in the *département* of the Dor-

dogne.) The tour de la Grosse Cloche is still often called the porte Saint-James, for it replaced an earlier twelfth-century gateway through which Compostela pilgrims passed on their way out of the city. Its clock was added only in 1759 and the great bell was hung here sixteen years later.

Beyond the gateway, rue Louis-Lande leads left to the four-teenth-century Gothic church of Sainte-Eulalie, one of whose door-ways is named after Saint-Jacques and was richly decorated in the six-teenth century. These treasures apart, it is above all the ancient church of Saint-Seurin, the oldest in this city, which is Bordeaux's greatest treasure. Present-day Saint-Seurin dates only from the eleventh century, and some of it, notably the façade, only from the nineteenth, but it stands on a much older building whose crypt was built in the fifth century by the very first Christians of the city. Saint-Seurin still cares for some of the relics of St Front, the evangelist of Périgord whom later mythology decided had been one of the seventy-two followers of Jesus mentioned in the Gospels. Some even alleged that he rode all the way from Jerusalem to this part of France on a camel. Amongst his powers (even in death) are those of reviving feeble children, whose mothers in Bordeaux – so the verger insists – still pray to him for this purpose.

Saint-Seurin preserves memories of the pilgrimage to Compostela, not because of any image of St James but because of its connection with the legend of Roland and Oliver. After Roland had vainly tried to summon help against the Moors, Charlemagne is said to have reverently laid his hero's useless horn in its crypt. The ivory horn was useless not only because Roland had blown it too late to summon help, but also because when he finally brought himself to sound it, he blew so hard that the ivory horn split in two.

Romantic ruins: all that remains of the late medieval church of St. Jacques
at Orleans.

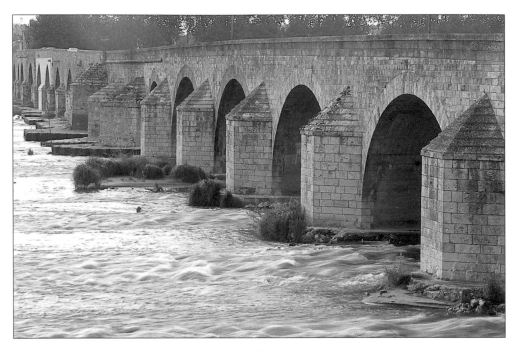

Above The eleventh century bridge at Beaugency was built specifically for the use of pilgrims to Santiago de Compostela.

Below A Romanesque-Gothic belfry is the sole survivor of the medieval church of St. Martin, Tours, which was replaced by this basilica.

Above A statue of St. Catherine of Alexandria in the church at Sainte-Catherine-de-Fierbois.

Right At Poitiers pilgrims still visit the church at Saint-Hilaire-le-Grand.

Below Aimery Picaud worshipped here at Parthenay-le-Vieux.

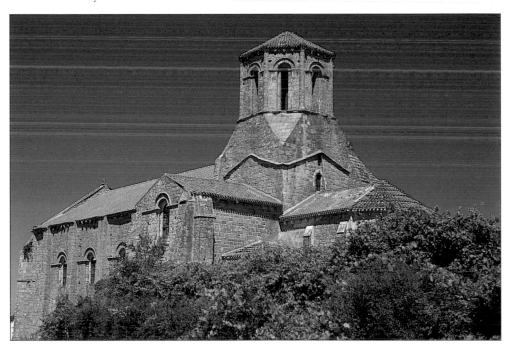

Above Once a Roman capital known as Mediolanum Santorum, Saintes still preserves its ancient amphitheatre.

Below Here, at Blaye, in 1526 King François of France came to venerate the remains of Charlemagne's peer Roland.

Above Sculpted angels surround the enthroned Jesus over the entrance to the church of Saint-André at Sauveterre-de-Béarn.

Below The fortified bridge at Sauveterre-de-Béarn stops half-way across the River Oloron. The rest was once spanned by a drawbridge.

At Saint-Jean-Pied-de-Port the flowery balconies, medieval bridge and
belfry of Notre-Dame-du-Bout-du-Pont are reflected in the River Nive.

Above The church and
monastic buildings at
Roncesvalles, zinc-roofed
against the rigours of
winter.

Right A fourteenth
century pilgrim's cross
stands just outside
Roncesvalles.

Ogival arches span the delicate Spanish Renaissance cloisters of the
monastery of Santa Maria la Real at Nájera.

CHAPTER THREE

FROM BORDEAUX TO THE PYRENEES

BORDEAUX – ARCACHON – BELIN-BÉLIET – PISSOS – LIPOSTHEY –
MARQUÈZE – DAX – SAINT-VINCENT-DE-PAUL – TERCIS-LES-BAINS –
POUILLON – PEYREHORADE – SORDE-L'ABBAYE – SAUVETERRE-DE-BÉARN
– SAINT-PALAIS – SAINT-JEAN-PIED-DE-PORT.

N EAR THE RAILWAY STATION at Bordeaux I stayed in a
one-star hotel where the concierge spoke English with a Scots
accent. He was an agreeable companion, too, declaring that he preferred Glasgow to Bordeaux, save that there was no restaurant in the
hotel and I had to quit him to eat fish soup and also fish for my main
course in a restaurant along the street. The next morning I left the city
and like the medieval pilgrims soon reached Gradignan, where they
could stay in hospice of Cayac, founded in the twelfth century by the
Hospitallers of St John of Jerusalem. In the past I had already often
admired its splendid Gothic ruins, before driving directly south
along the N10 through the *département* of the Landes on my way to
Spain. This is a good road, but its seemingly endless rows of pine
forests become boring. On this pilgrimage I took the opportunity
frequently to leave the N10 and thread my way through the Landes
instead of leaving the *département* behind as fast as possible. My first
plan was to discover one of the curiously shifting sand-dunes which
we know greatly troubled medieval pilgrims, and so I made my way
for Arcachon, along the road which runs in a straight line south-west
through a regional natural park. Part of the reason for declaring this a
protected region is simply to encourage those who live here to stay
and cherish the land and its fragile ecology, for the countryside has
become depopulated and sadly neglected as families have found more
rewarding work elsewhere. The whole natural park embraces some
206,000 hectares, and it seemed to me a haven of peace.

The road began to skirt the Arcachon basin, which has become a
paradise for ornithologists. As a seaside resort Arcachon is excellent,
and as anything else is no great shakes in my view – though it boasts
some fine beaches and the sea certainly makes a spectacular incursion
into France at this point. The town scarcely existed before the coming

of the railway in 1857 opened up its beaches to tourists. Before then its church of Notre-Dame was revered by mariners because of a fifteenth-century marble statue of the Virgin Mary which became the centre of a pilgrimage held on the feast of the Annunciation. Interestingly enough, the paintings in the sacristy of this church are Spanish in origin. Once again, I guess, pilgrims returning from Santiago must have brought them.

My aim was to see a celebrated mountain of sand known as the Dune de Pilat, chiefly because of some remarks of the medieval pilgrims' guide Aimery Picaud. After observing how excellent was the wine and how abundant the fish of Bordeaux, he warned pilgrims now to expect neither bread nor wine, neither fish nor water nor wells. Villages, he pointed out, were rare in the sandy soil of the Landes, food was mostly poor, and the pilgrim would have to survive on honey, millet and pork. Then he added: 'If by chance you are crossing the Landes in summer, take care to protect your face from the enormous flying insects which they call wasps and gadflies.' And, as a further precaution, he urged his followers to watch where they put their feet, warning them that the sand was never still and it was easy to sink speedily in it as far as the knees.

The dune which I wished to see rises to a height of 115 metres, (higher than any other in Europe) nine kilometres to the south of Arcachon just beyond Pilat-Plage. What is more, in spite of the pines planted at its borders, the pile of sand – as Picaud warned – is continually growing and also moving, as the ocean brings in more of it and the winds blow. From what I took to be the summit of the Dune de Pilat I gazed across the forest, which ought to be able to contain the moving sand but evidently cannot. Many have suggested that in the past pilgrims traversing the Landes sank so far into such moving sand dunes that they were suffocated to death and never reached Compostela. From my own observations of the dune this seems an unlikely tale.

In planning to meander through the Landes forest I had already researched the names of several spots once (or still) considered specially holy or useful by pilgrims to Compostela. The N250 took me comfortably back east just south of the Arcachon basin and as far as the D5, where I turned south-east through the park. Pilgrims undoubtedly used this route, for it follows an ancient Roman road. As many of them must have done, I made a tiny excursion to Mios, for this is miracle country again, and Mios used to be renowned for its miraculous fountain, whose waters (so an informant insisted as we talked, sitting on a wall) still cure not only colics but also headaches. Was he, tongue in cheek, treating me as a credulous fool, I wondered?

Rejoining the D5, I met the N10 at Le Barp, where in the thirteenth century stood a pilgrims' hospice and where the church is still dedicated to Saint-Jacques. Unfortunately it was locked.

The road winds on for twelve kilometres to Salles, a pretty little spot washed by the River Eyre. So is Belin-Béliet, reputedly the birthplace of Eleanor of Aquitaine and my next stop. Here pilgrims to Compostela were certainly cared for in the Middle Ages, comforted no doubt by the sight of the feudal château whose remnants still jut up from its yet more ancient mound. Aimery Picaud alleged that Roland's companion Oliver was buried here, along with other heroes of the tragedy at Roncesvalles. The *Chanson de Roland* decreed otherwise, stating that Oliver lay buried alongside Roland at Blaye. The truth or otherwise of Picaud's assertion seems not to have mattered in the twelfth century, for Aimery also observes that a delicious scent emanated from the hero's tomb at Belin-Béliet, a scent so sweet that it could heal the sick.

My map indicated a spot named l'Hospitalet, situated just north of Belin-Béliet. If the name implies that there was once a hospice here, I failed to find it. So I turned back south, to be rewarded at Saugnacq-et-Muret with a delightful twelfth-century church containing not simply a series of cockle-shells sculpted in its woodwork but also a statue of St Roch, dressed in a pilgrim's hat and cloak, decorated with cockle-shells and clearly on his way to Santiago de Compostela.

Roch is one of my favourite saints, if only because his iconography portrays him invariably displaying an elegant leg. Born at Montpellier in France at the end of the thirteenth century, he went on a pilgrimage to Rome and discovered there a terrible plague. St Roch instantly decided to care for those who had been afflicted. He inevitably caught the disease himself. Happily a little dog looked after him, bringing the stricken Christian food stolen from its own master's table. Recovering from the plague, Roch discovered that he had been granted the power to heal others. After returning to his birthplace he died in gaol in Montpellier, stupidly imprisoned by his uncle, the lord of the city, who had failed to recognize him. In his statues and portraits Roch shows his leg (sometimes the left one, sometimes the right) in order to display a bubo of the plague. What is remarkable at Saugnacq-et-Muret (and this is a phenomenon I came upon later in my journey) is that although his own pilgrimage was to Rome, St Roch is here dressed as a pilgrim to Santiago.

My route now became more and more exciting, as I drove off left towards Moustey. The hamlet boasts a couple of churches sitting side by side like two aged ladies settling down for a chat. Why did such a spot need two churches? The answer is that one, the narrower of the two, is dedicated to Notre-Dame and served as the hamlet's parish church, while the other was built for the use of pilgrims. This church is dedicated to St Ives and St Martin of Tours, with one of its stained glass windows depicting our pilgrim saint, hatless but with his pilgrim's staff and bag over his shoulder. The alleged relics of St Ives inside the building are evidence that pilgrims on their way from Brittany to Compostela must often have passed this way. Pissos, six kilometres due south, was in some respects even more rewarding, for here stands a so-called *maison des artisans*, crammed with local style furniture, traditional wickerwork and ceramics. Its Romanesque church (with a belfry of 1681) houses some fourteenth-century frescoes depicting on the one hand the rewards of those who aid pilgrims and on the other the grisly destiny in hell of the selfishly sinful.

I drove due west along a road laid out by the Romans to rejoin the N10 at Liposthey, where I turned south. At Labouheyre, twelve kilometres to the south, the Carmelites built a convent in the twelfth century as a halt for pilgrims on their way to Santiago, which was then fortified against attack. The convent has gone, but the fortifications can still be seen, as well as a twelfth-century church dedicated to Saint-Jacques. As you travel further south the Landes change their character. A part of these immense forests have been planted and replanted over two centuries. So often were the woods ravaged by fire that nowadays gaps are left as fire-breaks, though the threat of destruction remains. Little rivers and unexpected clearings scarcely break what at first appears to be the monotony of the pine trees (some of them with buckets tied to them, collecting the dripping resin), though the medieval pilgrim must have found his progress even more tedious – and dangerous. The Landes were humid and inhospitable until in the eighteenth century new techniques of planting grass kept the sand dunes at bay and afforestation became possible.

Even then the peasants were too poor to carry out the massive task required of them. Napoleon Bonaparte on his way through the Landes in 1808 promised to transform the region into a garden, draining the swamps and marshlands which had been another hazard for pilgrims to Compostela. He failed to keep his promise. Passing through the region in the mid-nineteenth century visitors described it as a desert and a dead land. The people of the Landes have to thank not Bonaparte for improving their land and life but his nephew, Emperor Napoleon III. The Empress Eugénie, Napoleon's bride, had adored Biarritz since she had discovered at the age of twenty-one what was then no more than a fishing village. After their marriage in 1853 she and the emperor made the spot one of their five official residences, spending their summer holidays there each year and trans-forming the place into one of the most fashionable resorts in France. Her husband obviously caught Eugénie's delight in the south-west.

In 1857 Napoleon III brought in a law requiring the local authorities of the Landes to create proper drainage and to begin systematic planting of trees. What is more, the Emperor provided public funds to help, making the state responsible for roads and for planting the dunes. His personal interest caused him to buy up a large area for plantation, giving it the name Solférino to celebrate his victory over the Austrians at the battle of that name in June 1859. (In truth it was scarcely a victory, for the Austrians had simply withdrawn in the face of the troops of France and Sardinia-Piedmont, and Napoleon III made peace three weeks later.) The American civil war unexpectedly helped this region, for Europe was cut off from much American wood and resin, and this part of France seized the chance to fill the gap. Yet life remained hard here, especially after the demand for pit props declined in the 1930s.

One further curiosity dating from the time of Napoleon III and the Empress Eugénie is another odd name in the Landes: Mexico. Bestowed in 1863 after the Mexican capital had capitulated before French forces in 1853, the name presaged a tragedy, for France then offered the Mexican throne to Maximilian, Archduke of Austria and brother of the Emperor Franz Joseph I. Maximilian foolishly accepted. When the French withdrew their forces, he was captured by enemy troops and shot. Mexico, though I could not find it on my map, turned out not to be far away from where I had reached, near Commensacq, a handful of kilometres to the right and washed by a stream known as the Grande Leyre.

An unexpected treat was in store. At Sabres, which boasts a luxu-riously decorated church with a Renaissance doorway, the ancient nineteenth-century railway station has been decorated to tempt tourists to ride in carriages of yesteryear, pulled by an even more antique locomotive along four kilometres of single track as far as the village of Marquèze. Some would prefer to walk and forbear the chil-dish pleasure of the ten-minute ride, but not I. (In any case, I am fairly certain that you are not allowed to walk, in case you damage the ecology; but that may be something I dreamed up.) Marquèze has become the home of the eco-museum of the natural park. In truth, I think it slightly too good to be true, for its well restored main house of 1824 has been joined by buildings brought here from other hamlets (a lambing shed, piggery, beehive, ancient oven and the rest). Still, the ensemble is pleasing, the vines have been replanted and the exhibition here realistically expounds what these forests and the Landes of the late nineteenth century looked like, and how the people worked or simply seemed to stalk about on stilts. Yet elsewhere in this region I still preferred to wander through the forests and find for myself the often tumbledown but agreeable farmhouses, most of them one-storey, with long tiled roofs sloping up to a central point.

Even those who enjoy forests will probably concede that further south the Landes become much more attractive. The terrain transforms itself from sand dunes to good farming land, and the countryside begins to undulate pleasantly. Chickens peck and cattle graze in pastures alternating with land used for sowing. Yet, curiously enough, the inhospitable upper Landes as well as the friendlier lower Landes were fiercely fought over during the centuries after the Roman legions withdrew. The Visigoths became rulers of the countryside, bequeathing their name (from the local version *Vascons*) both to the Gascons and to the Basque country. Next the seventh-century Arab invasions of France troubled the territory. I made my way from Sabres through this now peaceful and still strangely isolated part of France by way of Solférino back to the N10. Twenty-five kilometres south-west I reached Castets and turned south-east to reach the pilgrimage town of Dax.

Though its centre is extremly posh, its environs are fairly nasty. On the way into the city, at Sant-Paul-lès-Dax, I spotted the carved Romanesque apse of the parish church. In an animated line, bearded men stand between swirling grapes, some of the men carrying the kind of tools that must have carved this scene in the late eleventh or early twelfth century.

The city itself came as a complete surprise to me. Where else, I asked myself, had I seen this blend of mini-hospitals, exquisitely manicured parks, artificial pools, fountains, streams and clipped gardens? Dax also obviously sets itself up to entertain its visitors royally. *Foie gras* and other supposedly gastronomic meals were on offer (although a *pot au feu* of leeks, turnips, onions, ham, veal, parsley, carrots and garlic seemed to me, though very welcome, scarcely out of this world as a culinary masterpiece). Dax is a city of some pretensions, far more resembling say Baden-Baden in Germany or Buxton in Great Britain than a staging-post on the pilgrimage route to Santiago de Compostela, for this is a flourising spa.

At Dax virtually the only present-day hint of its antiquity is the Latin derivation of its name (meaning place of waters or *d'aquae*). The Romans relished the abundant thermal waters around what they called Aquae Tarbellicae (and then Aquae Augustae), and Dax still prospers on their reputation. Today the city is France's second most important spa after Aix-les-Bains. The main spring gushes some two million, four thousand litres of water a day at a temperature of 64 degrees centigrade. The water from this *fontaine chaude* serves thirteen thermal establishments in the city. It used to be called *La Néhé*, the name of the local Roman goddess who was supposed to look after it. Today, in these waters and in mud baths, visitors appease the pains of rheumatism or sooth broken or twisted limbs, before plunging into swimming pools said to be equally therapeutic.

What of medieval pilgrims? Architecturally I found scarcely anything they might have seen. Prosperity enables us foolishly to destroy the inheritence of the past, and in the eighteenth century Dax rebuilt its cathedral, retaining only a beautiful thirteenth-century portal from its Gothic predecessor. I was equally disappointed in this same quest at the hamlet of Saint-Vincent-de-Paul (formerly known as Pouy), which lies nine kilometres away to the north-east and was the birthplace in the 1570s or 1580s of the celebrated Monsieur Vincent, the great French saint and philanthropist. After being caught on a sea-voyage by brigands, Monsieur Vincent became a galley-slave. His demeanour so impressed his master that the future saint was released and thenceforth devoted himself to the care of anyone in need. The Thirty Years' War impoverished thousands, and the followers of Monsieur Vincent succoured them, eventually becoming known as the Lazarists and Daughters of Charity. At the hamlet of Saint-Vincent-de-Paul even the house in which he was born was demolished and had to be reconstructed after his canonization in the eighteenth century. The church dedicated to him turns out to be a completely out-of-place Byzantine construction built in 1864. Nevertheless the hamlet does have its charms, surrounded by oak trees and the pastures where as a boy the future saint guarded his father's flocks. His favourite oak was so cut up by pilgrims who took away pieces of it that today it is protected by a wall and grill.

My map revealed a sanctuary five kilometres further to the north-east called Notre-Dame-de-Buglose, and here I had more luck, even though the hamlet's fifteenth-century statue of the Virgin Mary is housed in what I thought an unpleasant modern church (with a carillon of sixty-four bells). Until the wars of religion she stood not in this church but in a little chapel beside a spring reputed to work miraculous cures. Chapel and spring appear at the end of an alley of plane trees, and the spring is probably just as likely to cure one's rheumatism as the more expansive thermal waters in Dax itself.

Whether or not pilgrims to Compostela in the past would have been drawn to such spots, the main thrust of their route from Dax ran south. I left the city by way of boulevard Carnot, wondering where I might stay the night. The late nineteenth-century church of Saint-

Vincent-de-Xaintes along the boulevard made me pause, to be rewarded with a fragment of Dax's antiquity, for along with some ancient sarcophagi it shelters a mosaic discovered nearby and said to be Gallo-Roman. Then I drove on and found the Hôtel Saint-Christophe at Tercis-les-Bains.

As I sat drinking a carafe of wine and waiting for my meal at this excellent unpretentious hostelry I spotted that I was nearing Spain, for on the wall were last year's posters advertising the arrival of Spanish matadors to perform in the bullrings of Dax. Sangria was also on sale here, billed as 'a ray of sun in your glass'.

Suggesting to the proprietress that this part of France was less savage than Spain in hosting bullfights without actually slaying the animals, I was surprised when she told me that of course they are killed. 'A pity,' I suggested. 'Not at all,' she replied, 'It's no different from slaughtering them in the abattoir.' Personally I do think the practices are quite different, but my meal had arrived, so I declined to say so, simply taking comfort from the information she volunteered that the bulls fight back: the one local matador was lying in hospital, seriously gored. Then, having spoken to me of bloodthirstiness, she demurely poured the remnants of another party's water jug into a vase of flowers.

Medieval pilgrims habitually stayed not here but at Pouillon, some fifteen kilometres south-west of Dax, so the next morning I wound a tortuous though extremely pleasant way, through woods and valleys and past lakes, to what is today a charming village. Founded as a Roman camp, Pouillon boasts a Romanesque church which was soon fortified for the protection of those stopping here. The glamorous high altar obviously dates from the eighteenth century, but an inscription in Latin on the wall behind it gives the information that the church was consecrated in 1045. From here I twisted south-west, through equally lovely country with some fine views, to Cagnotte, the local patois for 'little dog', a name deriving from the animal nestling at the feet of a statue of the Blessed Virgin Mary which once graced its Romanesque abbey church of Notre-Dame. Today the statue has disappeared, but the church still shelters the tombs of several of the former viscounts of the *pays d'Orthe*, a line dating from the early eleventh century. The church also turned out to house a sixth-century font and a remarkable sarcophagus hewn out of beechwood.

The countryside is now exceedingly attractive. I was no longer driving through flatlands, and the relentless pines had been replaced by more varied woods, with trees rising on either side of the road as it wound through the undulating land. Seven kilometres south-west of

Cagnotte I reached Peyrehorade (whose name, I discovered in a local guide-book, means 'stone with holes in it'). It was Wednesday morning, and the market was bustling away – the heir of one authorized by King Edward III of England in 1357 when the Plantaganets ruled this part of France. The whole town is still guarded by the Château de Aspremont which rises by the riverside. Though much of this château was built in the sixteenth century on behalf of Adrien d'Aspremont, Viscount of Orthe, the squat pepperpot towers at each corner of the high-roofed building seem to me scarcely to nod towards the transformation from fortress to comfortable residence that was taking place elsewhere during this and the previous century.

Peyrehorade is the capital of the pays d'Orthe, which covers the extent of the former viscounty. Though the region is still officially part of the Landes, it seems altogether another part of the world. Maize is grown to feed the ducks and geese, as well as (in winter) the white cattle which I increasingly saw feeding in the meadows. This has been maize country for centuries, and its sale was so profitable that the crop used to be transported along the River Adour as far as Bayonne. Aimery Picaud, however, issued a warning to his fellow pilgrims about this river traffic. Should they be tempted to ask a lift across one of the many rivers of the region in one of the local boats, they ought to remember first that the ruffians who owned them were rapacious enough to demand a coin for a foot passenger and four times as much for a horse. Next, declared Picaud, the boats were miserable affairs, hewn out of tree-trunks and likely to tip both pilgrim and horse into the river. He recommended clambering only into a boat that was half-empty and forcing the horses to wade across the river after it.

The monks who sheltered pilgrims helped to foster the profitable farms of the pays d'Orthe. Across the River Gave and a couple of kilometres south-west of Peyrehorade the abbey of Arthous rises amid the maize field and woods. The Premonstratensian monks who founded it in the twelfth century directly on the route to Compostela deliberately intended their abbey as a staging post for pilgrims. It flourished for centuries and then was savagely ruined during the wars of religion. The abbey regained its prosperity in the eighteenth century, only to be sacked at the Revolution and left to decline. To my surprise I found it in far better condition than I had expected, with parts of it exceedingly well restored. Happily, too, the apse of the original Romanesque church remains intact. Inside the nave, in three pieces, lies what was once the sculpted tympanum of the west door, depicting the adoration of the Magi.

I drove back to the river and turned right along the D29 towards

Sorde-l'Abbaye, which lies but three kilometres from Peyrehorade. Sorde-l'Abbaye has a complicated history. It developed as a fortified *bastide* around a monastery founded here by Benedictines on what had been the site of a Gallo-Roman villa. Its ramparts, today ivy-covered and with occasional doors let into them beside the original arches, date from the thirteenth century. The church itself is fortified, built out of bands of brick and stone, with massive buttresses and scarcely a window letting light (or intruders) into its lower parts. Today the Romanesque carvings on the church porch are badly muti-lated, but you can still make out Christ in majesty and spot how the masons cunningly used differently hued stones to enhance their work on the building. Did I discern the bull symbolizing St Mark and per-haps the beak of an eagle which once represented St John, or was this wishful thinking? Certainly on the arch of this doorway you can make out carvings of the wise and foolish virgins who were awaiting the return of their Lord. Five of them are taking good care of their lamps, whilst the five following ones lose theirs.

I stepped down into the three-aisled interior of the abbey church, admiring the finely carved capitals below its pointed arches and try-ing to imagine from their perfectly preserved selves what the portal must have looked like in the past. As evidence of the antiquity of Sorde-l'Abbaye, the choir of this church incorporates an intricately designed Gallo-Roman mosaic, with a dog chasing a rabbit, and other animals and birds busily staring at each other. When I came out and bought myself some black-skinned cheese, I was also told that if I went inside the fomer abbot's house (which overlooks the River Olo-ron) I would discover the remains of a Gallo-Roman spring. But I failed to find my way inside.

Like the church, the village that grew up around it is also fortified, the result of an agreement of 1290 between the abbot and King Philippe IV of France that Sorde-l'Abbaye should be transformed into a *bastide*. From this once-threateningly defensive but today en-chanting spot I drove back a little way towards Peyrehorade and then turned left along the little D123 to reach the T-junction of the main road. This now took me south-east, meandering through sleepy vil-lages and hamlets for its twenty-one kilometres to Sauveterre-de-Béarn. The Béarn is a gentle, green and wooded country whose streams drive modest mills. Occasional herds of yellow cattle grazed in the pastures.

Sauveterre-de-Béarn dominates the River Oloron at its con-fluence with the Mauléon. Here the pilgrims once possessed their own hospice. The stepped walls and the evocative medieval ensemble of the town appeared as I crossed the bridge over the Oloron and wound up to the centre. At the heart of the fortified town, the Romanesque church of Saint-André boasts above its triple apse a crenellated tower which looks more like a keep than a belfry, as well as a splendid main doorway, in excellent condition partly because it is protected by a portico and partly because of nineteenth-century restoration. Its porch bears an arcade of sculpted angels and a mandorla in which is depicted Christ in majesty. Jesus is surrounded by the symbols of the four evangelists and also by the sun and the moon. The pillars inside are decorated not simply what the stylized leaf forms that you expect to find in such churches but also with far more complex Romanesque capitals than usual. That on the pillar to the left of the apse I found the most delightful, depicting the vices of greed and scandal-mongering.

The town is crammed with medieval houses, gateways and manors, all guarded by the remains of its thirteenth-century fortifications and the rectangular keep of the ruined Château de Montréal, which rises sheer from the cliffs. Even the narrow medieval bridge is bazzarely fortified. Though it was built in the eleventh century, we owe its present form to Viscount Gaston Febus of Béarn, who ruled the region in the late fourteenth century. He changed his name to Febus in homage to the sun-god, whose rays he believed paralleled the spread of his realms and also matched his own golden hair. Partway across the bridge is a defensive keep. And the bridge itself stops halfway across the river, the rest of the water once being spanned by a drawbridge. The drawbridge survived until 1512, when King Jean d'Albret of Navarre had it demolished as a precaution against a Spanish invasion. Legend recounts that when the beautiful widow of Viscount Gaston v of Béarn was accused of killing her own child, born deformed after her husband's death in 1170, her brother put her to trial by ordeal. Hands and feet tied, she was flung from the bridge into the river. The waters bore her gently and unharmed to the bank, thus apparently proving her innocence, and Gaston's widow was restored to all her former rights.

Recrossing the River Oloron, from Sauveterre-de-Béarn I twisted my way south-west to Saint-Palais, which lies on the old Roman route from Bordeaux in France to Astorga in Spain. Just outside Sauveterre-de-Béarn the road crosses the River Saison, a tributary of the Oloron, at Osserain where pilgrims to Compostela could find another hospice. The hospice has gone, but the picturesque old quarter of Osserain, with its narrow alleyways, is still known as the *quartier de l'Hôpital*. What does remain is a fourteenth-century inn, vestiges of the fourteenth-century abbey of Saint-Elix and a seventeenth-century château with a tower built four centuries earlier.

Even before I reached Saint-Palais the peaks of the Pyrenees, the border with Spain, rose ahead of me. To my delight the information office at the Mairie of Saint-Palais informed me that part of the exhibition of the town's local history museum was dedicated to Saint-Jacques of Compostela. This turned out to be the kind of exhibition that pleases me most, full enough to be worth visiting, small enough not to wear out the feet of the most fainthearted museum-crawler. Amongst its exhibits are copies of the coats of arms of the principal towns of Lower Navarre, seventeen of them including cockle-shells. Photographs of yesterday's pilgrims showed these too festooned with shells, wearing hats with turned-up brims and bearing staffs. Here also is displayed a copy of the Codex Callixtus, in which Aimery Picaud's celebrated guide was discovered. Finally the exhibition includes copies of fascinating impressions of St James which I had never come across, including one by (of all painters) the rococo master of aristocratic playfulness, Jean-Antoine Watteau. The representation I least liked is a modern statue by the Navarre sculptor José Ulibarrena, in which the saint holds a cockle-shell that resembles an ill-fitting glove.

Saint-Palais lies in the realms of the former Kingdom of Navarre, and a photograph here sent me looking for another ancient house in the town. In the seventeenth century, portrait medallions of the three last sovereigns of the kingdom – Henri II, Jeanne III d'Albret and Henri IV – were carved on one of its walls. The helpful assistant at the local history museum directed me out of the Mairie, with instructions to turn immediately left and left again at the church. The house, she said, is the second on the right at the end of that street. I could not initially spot the busts, simply because they are set high up on the building, so I walked back to the post office and asked for more help from the staff. No one at the counter expressed any knowledge of these portraits. Such is the fate of three of the greatest sovereigns of this part of France. Henri II d'Albret was the monarch who tried in vain in 1521 to regain that part of his kingdom south of the Pyrenees which the Spanish had conquered. Five years later he married the sister of François I, King of France. In 1553 their daughter Jeanne III d'Albret gave birth to the man who was to become one of the successors of François on the French throne and (in the eyes of many historians) amongst the greatest of the Kings of France.

The future Henri IV of France was baptized with a drop of Jurançon wine mingled with a clove of garlic. Before becoming King of France he took the thrones of Béarn (as Henri II) and of Navarre (as Henri III). This was the era of the wars of religion, and Henri was brought up by his mother as a Calvinist. In 1572 he would have been murdered by the Catholics, but for professing to have changed sides. Three years later he renounced his forced conversion and took command of the Protestant army. Henri of Navarre was next in line for the French throne when King Henri III was assassinated in 1589. Most Catholics, the majority of the French nation, objected. Three years later, having virtually annihilated the forces of his enemies, Henri took the judicious step of declaring himself a Catholic, with the celebrated remark, 'Paris is worth a Mass.' His rule as Henri IV was one of such careful management of the French economy that the country prospered and was opened up to trade, above all by the building of new roads throughout the kingdom. Nevertheless, in 1610 a Jesuit fanatic named Ravaillac assassinated him.

He and his two ancestors look down from the medallions of this humble house in Saint-Palais, Henri II with his staring eyes, Jeanne d'Albret with braided hair and bare breasts, and Henri IV with an immense hooked nose. Beside them are the busts of an unknown woman and a man with a horrible-looking face.

From Saint-Palais the road towards Spain climbs and dips and climbs again. The trees become sparser, and herds of cows have long been replaced by flocks of black-faced sheep. At Uhart-Mixe, with its seventeenth-century château, three major French routes to Compostela – from Paris, Vézelay and Le Puy – came together in order to cross the Pyrenees. A stele carved with the Maltese and other crosses marks the spot, its granite plinth designed by Dr Clément Urrutibéhety of Saint-Palais and incised with the staff and bag of St James. I was driving not too fast, but at the bottom of the next dip I almost missed the sign pointing right to Harambels. The village well merited a visit. In the Middle Ages the Benedictines staffed a priory and pilgrims' hospice here, dedicated to St Nicolas. Its twelfth-century Romanesque chapel has survived. Over the door of the chapel is inscribed a five-pointed star and another Maltese cross, symbol of the Hospitallers who once guarded the pilgrims from danger and gave them shelter. Inside the chapel I was astonished to find a gilded seventeenth-century retable, its pilasters decorated with vines. This retable is decorated with an anecdote from the life of St Nicolas, over which Jesus reigns from the cross, succoured by his mother and St James of Compostela. Although the statue of James is in a sorry state, having lost his right arm and been severely battered over the centuries, you can still make out the cockle-shells on his mantle and hat.

Returning th the D933 and continuing in the direction of Saint-Jean-le-Vieux, at the summit of another mound I was bounding along fast enough to overshoot another road sign pointing right, this time to Ostabat, and I remain glad that I turned back to visit this little hamlet perched on its knoll. Again an apparently nonedescript place was once an important staging-post on the Roman road from Bordeaux to Astorga, the road which most pilgrims to Compostela followed. In the Middle Ages two major hospices stood here, as well as numerous other inns which altogether, it is said, could house 500 pilgrims. Vestiges of the ramparts of its fortress alone remain, for King Sancho the Strong of Navarre demolished them in the thirteenth century. Another ancient survival is a virtually indecipherable ancient inscription over the lintel of a barn. The barn doors were open, revealing that it is now used as a garage. I found no one at all around, so I could not enquire further as to the significance of it all.

The pilgrims' next stop, Saint-Jean-le-Vieux, was known as Uruttia until the fifteenth century. A fountain, dedicated to Saint-Jean-Baptiste-d'Urrutia, refreshed the pilgrims here, and they could worship in a church of the same dedication whose parish priest was appointed by the abbot of the Augustinian priory at Roncesvalles. I could find no traces of the fountain, but the ruins of the church of the same dedication can still be seen here on the left bank of the River Laurhibar. When Richard Coeur de Lion attacked the town in 1172, taking and destroying the Château de Saint-Per, his troops also despoiled the Romanesque church of Saint-Pierre, but they failed to ruin its Romanesque porch, and the building seems to me to have been most sensitively restored.

Finally I reached Saint-Jean-Pied-de-Port, the pilgrims' last stop before crossing into Spain. This was the place where I intended to stay overnight. Today it nestles at the foot of thirteenth-century, pink granite walls and at the approach to the Ibañeta pass (or *portcol*) from which it derives part of its name. According to the *Chanson de Roland*, after the battle of Roncesvalles Charlemagne ordered that the bodies of his slain peers be laid out here. In their memory, the legend continues, he then founded a monastery on the spot, dedicated to St John the Baptist.

This is probably an invention. Saint-Jean-Pied-de-Port achieved importance only after the late twelfth century, when the representatives of the Kings of Navarre in this region set up their headquarters in the Château de Mendiguren. They systematically developed the town in the next century, for example granting it the right to hold a market. Soon pilgrims were pressing on from Saint-Jean-le-Vieux to Saint-Jean-Pied-de-Port in order to stay in its more prestigious hospices. The citizens knew how to make them feel welcome, dubbing the gate by which they entered Saint-Jean-Pied-de-Port the porte Saint-Jacques and ringing the bells of the churches whenever a large contingent arrived. Pilgrims proceeded solemnly up the present rue de la Citadelle, sometimes being offered food by the locals as they passed. then they would find rest either in the hospice attached to the lovely Gothic church of Notre-Dame-du-Bout-du-Pont or the one served by the former church of Sainte-Eulalie-d'Ugange, of which only a fragmentary Romanesque doorway remains.

The citizens of Saint-Jean-Pied-de-Port were not welcoming these pilgrims simply out of the goodness of their hearts. At the local history museum of Saint-Palais I had bought a learned pamphlet by the same Dr Urrutibéhety which gives much entertaining information about how the people of Navarre (and especially the sovereigns) reaped a rich reward from their position on the route to Compostela. For instance, all the towns along the route soon began charging pilgrims tolls for the right to pass through, adjusting them in proportion to the wealth the pilgrim was carrying on his or her person. A German pilgrim, Arnold von Harff of Cologne, complained at the end of the fifteenth century that he had been thus charged at Saint-Palais and then again at Saint-Jean-Pied-de-Port. 'All this is given to the King of Navarre,' he expostulated, 'which seems to me an abuse, for I have never seen any other customs duty of this kind either in Christendom or in the lands of the Muslims.'

Other pilgrims were more generous. Count Raymond of Toulouse, on his return from Compostela in 1232, gave lands to the hospice at Roncesvalles worth twenty livres a year in recognition of the welcome the monks had shown him. Arnaud Raymond, Seigneur of Mixe-Ostabat, intending to set off soon for Compostela, made a will on 31 March 1312, bequeathing lands, vineyards and money to churches and hospices on the pilgrim route. He signed his will just in time for them to benefit, dying on 6 April without even setting off for Spain. Some pious sovereigns were even able to reward staging posts *en route* to Compostela at the expense of their subjects rather than themselves. So in 1472 Jean II of Aragon ordered several of his subjects to pay jointly to the churches and hospice of Saint-Palais an annual rent of a hundred livres. Ownership of such a strategic and wealth-creating town as Saint-Jean-Pied-de-Port was so much disputed between France and Spain that the French eventually decided to defend it by a citadel (which still stands) designed by the great Vauban himself.

Saint-Jean-Pied-de-Port remains exquisite, lying amid tree-covered slopes, its waters overhung by balconies leaning from whitewhashed walls. I arrived on a Monday when the market, descended from that granted in the thirteenth century, was in full fling. The town seemed also in my eyes a tourist trap, still keen to lift a fair amount of cash from the pockets of its visitors, so I changed my mind about staying overnight there and went back to Saint-Jean-le-Vieux. Aimery Picaud himself confessed that he disliked the people of Navarre, and not solely for their rapacity; but on the evidence of that one stay at Saint-Jean-le-Vieux I cannot say I found the villagers remotely, as he put it, wild, dishonest, corrupt, vain or even (as he attempted to prove by giving several indelicate examples of their behaviour) debauched.

In the morning, wondering what sort of Spanish wine I would soon encounter, I bought a case of French white Jurançon. It was an unnecessary precaution.

CHAPTER FOUR

FROM RONCESVALLES TO THE REALMS OF SANTIAGO MATAMAROS

Saint-Jean-Pied-de-Port – Valcarlos – Puerta de Ibañeta –
Roncesvalles – Burguete – Pamplona – Puente la Reina – Estella –
Irache – Torres del Rio – Viana – Logroño – Navarette – Najéra
– Santo Domingo de la Calzada – San Juan de Ortega – Burgos.

I LEFT Saint-Jean-Pied-de-Port by the Spanish gateway. The River
Nive here is crossed by a Roman bridge, and a little sign points up
the hillside towards Arnéguy. This was the chief route used by pilgrims to Compostela from the thirteenth century onwards. Aimery
Picaud preferred them to take the ancient Roman road, which
climbed much higher as it crossed over the mountains. 'This
mountain is so high that in truth it seems almost to touch the sky,' he
declared, 'and when you climb it you believe that you can do the
same.' He also recounted the legend that from the summit Charlemagne knelt and prayed facing not towards Jerusalem, as was the
custom of pilgrims till then, but towards Santiago de Compostela.

I had no choice but to follow the lower road, for the upper one
will not take motor vehicles. So I passed through Arnéguy, with its
mid-sixteenth century Basque church and its splendid views, and
then was waved through the Spanish frontier. My patron saint Saint-
Jacques de Compostelle had now become Santiago de Compostela. A
tributary of the Nive, known as the Nive d'Arnéguy, flows back into
France through the gorge of Valcarlos. As I left behind the waterfront
tranquillity of Saint-Jean-Pied-de-Port and start climbing up
through the Spanish village of Valcarlos towards the Ibañeta pass, the
pace seemed to quicken as the heroes of the past started to haunt the
route. The road winds up the narrow gulf through forests of chest-
nuts and beeches and oak trees, with the cliff falling away to one side.
The only cause of delay were slowly-climbing trucks filled with huge
tree-trunks, the only hazard being hikers, cyclists and mountain

goats who needed to be given their rightful space as they sweated along the route.

Valcarlos means the valley of Charles, and to evoke the name of Charlemagne here calls to mind more than anywhere else the most moving legend of the whole pilgrimage way to Compostela – the saga of Roland and Oliver. This is where in the year 778 they met their treacherous deaths at the hands of the Moors. As I sat on a February morning watching dancers performing among the gentle houses of the village of Valcarlos, which rise sweetly up the green hillside, the peaceful scene seemed to belie the savagery of the Roland saga. So does the heroic poem which the Norman cleric composed about the massacre four centuries after the event. I recalled a remark of Hilaire Belloc, who passed this way seventy years ago or so, that 'any man who may yet believe (I know such a discussion is pedantry) – any man who may yet believe the song of Roland to have been a Northern legend had better come to this place and drink the mountains in. For whoever wrote –

> High are the hills and huge and dim with cloud,
> Down in the deeps, the living streams are loud,

had certainly himself stood in the silence and majesty of this valley.'

The *Chanson de Roland* opens so stirringly that at this point I ought to quote the original before translating it:

> *Carles li reis nostre emperere magnes*
> *Set anz tuz pleins ad estet en Espaigne*
> *Conquist la tere tresque en le mer altaigne*
> *Ni ad castel ki devant lui remaigne*
> *Murs ne citez est remes a fraindre.*
> (King Charlemagne our emperor
> Has been seven full years in Spain,
> Conquered the land even to the high seas,
> No castle holds out against him,
> No wall or city is left to capture.)

Beginning with this proud boast before going on to describe the deaths of Roland, Oliver and the twelve peers of France, the poem bristles with ironies. Roland's headstrong courage makes him prevent Oliver blowing his horn to summon help before it is too late. Oliver at last calls for aid. Blood, mortally flowing down into his eyes, has blinded him. When Roland rides up to him, Oliver cannot recognize his friend and, taking him for an enemy strikes him a mighty blow with his sword. Roland's response is profoundly courteous.

> *Sun cumpaignum cum il l'ad encuntret*
> *Sil fiert amunt sur lélme a or gemmet*

> *Tut li detrenchet d'ici que l nasel*
> *Mais en la teste ne l'ad mie adeset.*
> *A icel colp l'ad Rollanz reguardet*
> *Si li demandet dulcement et suef*
> *'Sire cumpainz, faites le vus de gred?'*
> (When Oliver encounters his friend,
> He strikes down on the gemmed gold helmet,
> Splitting it from crown to nose,
> But his thrust fails to reach the head.
> At this blow Roland looks at him
> And gently and softly asks him,
> "Sire companion, was that in earnest?" '

When Charlemagne and his host rush back, the Moors retreat, leaving Oliver and his companions dead, and Roland dying. Roland feels a Moor attempting to filch his sword Durendal. Slaying the Moor with his ivory horn, Roland next tries in vain to smash Durendal on the grey rocks whose descendants still litter the pass. All that is left for Charlemagne is to avenge his heroes, putting those who betrayed them to death and, legend has it, burying Roland, Oliver and their dead companions at one of another half-a-dozen places I had already passed through on my own pilgrimage.

Not all of this is myth, but much is, the greatest calumny being to blame the Moors for the deaths of Roland and the emperor's rearguard, for historically they were slaughtered by avalanches of rocks thrown down on them by the people of Navarre, who were bent on avenging the sack of Pamplona. A second legendary element, as the astute Hilaire Belloc observed, is that the *Chanson de Roland* made them fall on the far side of the summit, upon the fields of Roncesvalles, with the sun setting right at them along the hills. Belloc added, 'And that is how it should be, for it is evident that (in a poem) the hero fighting among hills should die upon the enemy's side of the hills.' But that is not the place where Roland really died, Belloc argued. 'The place where he really died', he judged, 'was here in the very recess of the Northern valley. It was here only that rocks could have been rolled down upon an army, and here is that narrow, strangling gorge where the line of the march could most easily have been cut in two by the fury of the mountaineers.'

Medieval legend came to picture Roland's sovereign Charlemagne as the first ever pilgrim to Santiago. As they climbed up to Roncesvalles, pilgrims in the Middle Ages recounted (as today's pilgrims should surely still recount to themselves) the story of the *Chanson de Roland*, imagining a mythical Charlemagne leaving the buried bodies of his heroes and himself climbing to the top of the hill to set up a crucifix. It faced not towards Jerusalem but towards Santiago de Compostela – the same direction faced by Charlemagne when he knelt to pray.

The pass or Puerta de Ibañeta is 1057 metres above sea-level. On the way to it I noticed signposts directing winter skiers to their slopes and realized how suddenly high I had come. At the pass itself Charlemagne is said to have founded a monastery, with a pilgrims' hospice. Certainly one existed here in the twelfth century, by which time it was being called the monastery of Roland. In the religious disputes of the sixteenth century it was ruined. Rebuilt, it was again despoiled at the time of the French Revolution. Rebuilt a third time, it was burnt down in 1884. How long will the present church last? It dates only from 1965 and is dedicated to San Salvador. It stands on a spot where in the late eleventh century a hermit set up his cell simply to toll a bell throughout the night and in misty weather in order to point pilgrims along their way. Next to it is a stele sculpted with a copy of the thirteenth-century statue of the Madonna who sits on the high altar of the church as Roncesvalles. The inscription on the stele is in Basque, French and Spanish, and urges all pilgrims to sing a Hail Mary in honour of the Roncesvalles Madonna. Underneath it is a curious image: a crozier surrounded by chains. The chains refer to the spoils of battle taken by Sancho the Strong of Navarre who in 1212, fighting along Alfonso VIII of Castile, broke the military might of the Moors at the battle of Las Navas de Tolosa.

Within a few moments I reached Roncesvalles, the grey walls of which seem to me still to exude the melancholy, inspiring aura of the *Chanson de Roland*. This is the spot where, more than anywhere else on our pilgrimage, I also feel in my bones the apostle of the Prince of Peace being transformed into the slayer of the Moors, Santiago Matamoros, who appeared riding a white charger to inspire the Christians to victory at the battle of Clavijo. The Bishop of Pamplona, Sancho Larrosa, founded a convent here in 1132, and three years later Augustinian canons built one of the greatest hospices on the pilgrimage route. But the present church, dedicated to the Blessed Virgin Mary, was the gift of the same Sancho the Strong who slew enough Moors at Las Navas de Tolosa to merit the plaudits of Santiago Matamoros. He and his wife today lie in the fourteenth-century chapter house, reached through the monastery cloister, which was rebuilt in the seventeenth century. Sancho, who stood 2.20 metres tall, still lies in a massive Gothic tomb, the recumbent statue on top showing his eyes wide-open even in death. His wife was vouchsafed only a wooden one, which perished in the seventeenth century. I visited the monastic treasury to see an emerald worn, it is claimed, in the turban of a

Moorish leader slain by Sancho. Here too is displayed Sancho's massive armour, long said to be that of Roland himself, as well, as a fourteenth-century reliquary whose chequered patterns have earned it the soubriquet 'Charlemagne's chessboard'. The treasury proudly displays a twelfth-century document declaring that anyone, Christian or pagan, Jew, beggar or heretic, was to be welcomed at the hospice. Sancho the Strong's weapons are also on display, so huge that, like Sancho's armour, they were for many years supposed to have belonged to Roland himself.

The importance of Roncesvalles for the pilgrimage route is emphasized by the fact that the abbot of Sancho's monastery was to be chosen by the King of Navarre himself and to derive his authority not from any Spanish bishop but directly from the Pope. He was charged too with welcoming and caring both for the spiritual and the physical needs of pilgrims. Men and women, lodged separately, could take a bath here. For three days they were offered food and lodgings free of charge, while a surgeon, a doctor and an apothecary cared for the sick. There were hairdressers and, probably most important of all, cobblers to mend the pilgrims' boots. So great was the press of visitors at the end of the sixteenth century that the early twelfth-century inn had to be extensively remodelled and extended.

The monastery of Roncesvalles no longer displays the sternly delicate Romanesque aspect of the buildings which Sancho founded. Many times restored, today its buildings are basically Gothic, some of the first Gothic buildings of Spain in fact. The church is a three-aisled basilica with a balconied triforium. Inside is a thirteenth-century cedar-wood statue of the Blessed Virgin Mary, partly encased in silver, as is her infant Son, so that we can no longer admire the skills of the sculptor who made it. The statue, according to the legend, was carved by no human hand but discovered when men were led to a remote spot by a red deer in whose antlers shone a bright star. If you are there in May or June you can join the faithful from the surrounding villages in paying the image due homage. This church was ineptly restored in 1939, and I wish the restorers had run out of cash before they put in Munich stained glass.

The chapel of Espíritu Santo by the southern gate of the pilgrims' inn offers a more authentic glimpse of Romanesque Navarre than does the monastery. This is one of the earliest of the funerary chapels which dot the pilgrimage route through Navarre, for inevitably many pilgrims died before they reached their goal. Its square walls and arcaded gallery surround a huge underground ossuary, the whole created in 1140. Close by, the early Gothic church of Santiago reminds us that this is only one stage on our pilgrimage. It is worth pausing to admire the portrait of Christ in its porch. The bell in its tower is none other than that rung long ago by the hermit of the Ibañeta pass.

The roofs of the ecclesiastical buildings at Roncesvalles are made of zinc, since the winter weather can apparently penetrate any other material. As I passed through the village, workmen were constructing out of breeze-blocks the skeleton of what seemed to me a mock medieval castle. Rapidly passing it by I was more pleased to see the authentic fourteenth-century pilgrimage cross which a prior of Roncesvalles set up in 1880 to replace one destroyed by the marauding French in 1794.

Through hamlets and towns I descended from the heights of the Pyrenees. In one village a goat ran ahead of me and then darted straight into someone's home, where I presume he had his bed. Ancient Burguete was the first of the towns, the houses of its main street topped with sharply pointed roofs and decorated with coats of arms carved in stone. Burguete's own coat of arms incorporates a wild boar, evidence some say of the food its inhabitants offered to the pilgrims. Next I reached handsome, long El Espinal. Once the pilgrims could stay in a twelfth-century hospice, but today they must worship in the modern church of San Bartolomé before journeying on through rugged country to Viscarret. Here there is a little church whose Romanesque porch still survives. The hamlet of Larrasonaña today boasts a single street but once possessed another medieval hospice, perhaps the ancient building on the right at the entrance to the village which is inscribed with fading religious symbols. The church of St Nicolas, dating from the thirteenth century, once belonged to an Augustinian monastery.

Along the road dusty, windowless, ruined, aged churches and shrines stand on the hills. Then my route passed through unattractive suburbs until suddenly I was approaching the plateau of Pamplona. Though a built-up city, Pamplona still rises out of this plateau as Ernest Hemingway saw it some sixty years ago, with 'the walls of the city, and the great brown cathedral, and the broken skyline of the other churches.' As he recalled, 'In the back of the plateau were the mountains, and ahead the road stretched out white across the plain going towards Pamplona.' It still does.

The Basques, who helped Charlemagne to drive the Moors out of Pamplona, know this capital of Navarre as Iruña, whereas its Castilian name is a reminiscence of the Roman general Pompey, who founded it in the first century BC. It is easy enough to see why its site on the River Arga made Pamplona a much-prized stronghold, and the city still preserves its medieval fortifications. A Roman bridge crosses the river, whence you enter the city by the Portal del Francia, which is appropriately decorated with fleurs-de-lis.

I knew of this city only from Ernest Hemingway's novel *The Sun also Rises*. Since this was published a decade before I was born, my own copy happens to be the fourth printing (1957) of the Pan paperback edition, which seeks to inspire readers with the information that the novel is 'Now filmed with Ava Gardner and Tyrone Power'. Turning to the edition these days I marvel at the absurd blurb on the back cover of what is one of the twentieth-century's masterpieces of American literature:

> To love and be loved, yet to know fulfilment can never be achieved – that is Jake Barnes's tragedy.
>
> He and Brett Ashley drift about Paris, rootless, pleasure-seeking. She, attractive, passionate, can't resist the advances of other men.
>
> Together they go to Spain. Crowds flock to Pamplona's fiesta. Brett falls for a bull-fighter.
>
> 'I'm mad about him,' she tells Jake. 'I can't help it . . . It's tearing me all up inside.'

The book was in my car, and I sat in a café sipping Rioja and reading Hemingway's own description of the annual July bull-run through the streets of Pamplona. 'There were so many people running ahead of the bulls that the mass thickened and slowed up going through the gate into the ring, and as the bulls passed, galloping together, heavy, muddy-sided, horns swinging, one shot ahead, caught a man in the running crowd in the back and lifted him in the air. Both the man's arms were by his sides, his head went back as the horn went in, and the bull lifted him and then dropped him.' I have watched a bull-run at Béziers in the Languedoc, but reading Hemingway that day in Pamplona made me vow never to watch a bull-run again.

The oldest church of Pamplona recalls the saint to whose shrine I was bound. San Saturnino was built out of brick in the thirteenth century in a quarter peopled then by French merchants, after an earlier Romanesque building had been destroyed in 1275 during a conflict between Navarre and the citizens of Burgos. The present church was finished in 1297. One of its fortified towers is pierced only by slits. The other, with slightly arched openings revealing its bells and a staircase tower at one corner, makes a slightly greater attempt at graciousness but remains ultimately hostile and glowering. In the north porch is a statue of St James the Great, dressed as a pilgrim, with a pilgrim kneeling at his feet.

Another church, built in the sixteenth century and dedicated to Santiago himself, is also often called the church of San Domingo. It too houses a statue of the saint of Compostela. As for the cathedral which stands in the medieval quarter of this essentially modern town, its boring classical façade, insensitively added in the late eighteenth century by an architect named Ventura Rodriguez, should deter no one from visiting the exquisite flamboyant Gothic cloister, which was almost certainly built by French architects and masons. Attached to this cathedral is a medieval kitchen where food was cooked for the pilgrims on the way to Compostela. The great open chimney of this ancient building is flanked by four smaller ones. The cathedral refectory, for its part, is famous for its sculpted reliefs, in particular those which depict the scene where a young woman is tested for her virginity by being taken on horseback to meet a unicorn. The unicorn kneels before her, proof – according to the medieval bestiaries – that she is intact.

Though pilgrims might eat here, they would stay in the hospice that today houses a museum of Navarre. I stood gazing at it for a long time, for in the sixteenth century its façade was decorated with the first example of the plateresque style of architecture that I had so far come across on this journey. Plateresque means 'in the fashion of a silversmith'. The style consists of an excitingly overwrought mixture of ornament derived from Gothic, Renaissance and even Moorish patterns that bears little relationship to the structure of the building to which it is applied. This plateresque façade is virtually all that remains of Pamplona's pilgrims' hospice.

I drove on to Obanos, where a less violent annual spectacle than the bull-run of Pamplona takes place in the third week of August. The festival celebrates a princess of Aquitaine, St Félice, who after a pilgrimage to Compostela renounced her wealth and at nearby Amocáin devoted herself to a life of prayer. Unfortunately her brother Guilhem was so incensed by this decision that he hurried from France and slew his sister. Soon, however, he was filled with remorse, travelled to Compostela himself and then returned to do penance at the sanctuary where his sister was buried. Revered as a saint, Guilhem's remains lie buried here in the hermitage of Santa Maria Arnotegui.

Nearby are countless other dead bones of pilgrims to Compostela. Three kilometres east of Obanos I reached Eunate, where the Knights Templars established a monastery dedicated to Nuestra Señora de Eunate. Its octagonal Romanesque chapel stands isolated amidst green fields, its simple belfry designed to hold two bells but carrying only one. The church is surrounded by a quaint gallery which was used to shelter the pilgrims. What is more, Nuestra Señora de Eunate almost certainly served as one of the funeral chapels on the pilgrim route, so maybe it shelters the bones of pious St Félice.

The fortified town of Puente la Reina lies three kilometres due west of Eunate. Pilgrims entered the town by way of the church and monastery of the Crucifixion. In the mid-twelfth century the Templars ran this Iglesia del Crucifijo, selling bread and wine to pilgrims. Their demise allowed the church to fall into the hands of the Knights of St John of Jeruslam, who set up here a pilgrims' hospice, an architectural reminder of which are the scallop shells which make up the archivolts of the ogival doorway of the church. Fittingly, the Iglesia del Crucifijo at Puente la Reina houses a superb German Crucifixion brought here in the fourteenth century, presumably by a pilgrim from the Rhineland. Having venerated this image of the crucified Jesus, who is nailed to a Y-shaped tree, I next paused at the Romanesque church of Santiago itself. It stands to the right of the calle Maior, rebuilt in the sixteenth century and given a new tower in the eighteenth, but retaining the crumbling Romanesque porch which opens out on the street. The Moorish influence on its architecture is plain in the little Mozarabic arches which decorate this porch. Inside a baroque retable depicts the life of the patron saint. But I think the glory of this church is its fourteenth-century statue of Santiago. He stands barefooted, his beard curly as is his long hair, a staff in his left hand, the Scriptures in his right.

Fine Gothic houses, built in brick, line the narrow calle Maior which runs as far as the beautiful bridge that gave Puente la Reina its name. Built for pilgrims in the eleventh century, at the command of Doña Elvira, the wife of King Sancho III the Great of Navarre (or, as other historians assert, by Doña Estefania, wife of King Garcia of Najéra) its six irregular arches gracefully span the River Arga.

I have begun to think that along with a church dedicated to St James and a pilgrims' hospice, a medieval bridge is the third sign that I am following the old road to Compostela. Until the bridge was built at Puente la Reina the pilgrims had to wade through the river. A little further on they were warned by Aimery Picaud that fording the River Salado would poison their horses. Fortuntely I was able to drive over a modern bridge here and reach Estella safely.

The Romans founded Estella, and pilgrims tended to avoid it until 1090, when King Sancho I Ramirez decided to attract them there by bringing settlers here who (some say) were freemen and (others say) were Frenchmen (for the word *Francos* meant both). Soon churches, still extant, were built with dedications to the major French pilgrimage shrines of Rocamadour and Le Puy. Moreover, the water of the River Ega here was clean and refreshing, a fact noted by Picaud himself. He also praised its fresh bread, its wine, its meat and fish and its friendly welcome. Numerous pilgrims' hospices were established and inevitably flourished here. The Jews were welcomed for their financial acumen, accepted at Estella even when they were being expelled from other parts of Spain. Soon this increasingly prosperous town thought fit to rebuild the monastery and church of San Pedro de la Rua, which was proving too tiny for the burgeoning religious tourist trade. Pilgrims who died at Estella were often buried in its twelfth-century cloister, whose ancient beams and twin-columned arches still exude peace. Although I find the quarter of the town around San Pedro exquisite, perhaps the finest aspect of Estella is its setting, hilly country reflected in the steep steps which lead up to the twelfth-century church of San Miguel Arcángel, with its splendidly carved Romanesque north doorway. It depicts Christ in majesty in the style cultivated not by Spanish artists but by French sculptors from Poitou.

The very name of Estella is a reference to the star which allegedly revealed the site of the grave of Santiago. But so far as I discovered, St James and Charlemagne's paladin Roland are both depicted at Estella only once. Santiago appears in the magnificent fourteenth-century Gothic doorway of the church of the Holy Sepulchre (Santo Sepolcro), his bag and shells understandably worn since the time they were carved here in 1328. Roland puts in a more savage appearance. In the plaza de San Martin is a rare example of Romanesque civic architecture, the Palais Real, home of the Kings of Navarre who lived here in the twelfth century. Carved on one of its capitals, Roland does deathly battle with the Moorish champion Ferragut.

Violence is never far away on the road to Compostela. It puts in a second appearance no more than three kilometres further on at Irache, which is delightfully situated at the foot of Montejurra. Here in 1045 King Garcia Sánchez directed the abbot of the monastery of Santa Maria la Real to build a hospice for pilgrims to Santiago. The monastery itself is one of the oldest Benedictine foundations in Spain, established certainly in the tenth century. The present church is an entertaining mix of styles. Begun in the twelfth century, it was not finished till the sixteenth. I found Roland once again beating up Ferragut on a capital to the right of the choir. Irache flourished as a university town from 1569 to 1833, with students learning medicine, theology and art, but the needs of pilgrims were never neglected – so much so that one of the abbots, St Veremundo, is now the patron saint of Santiago pilgrims.

This stretch of my road to Santiago threw up delight after delight. The first was the little town of Los Arcos, whose monumental seventeenth-century gateway protects no more than 2,000 inhabitants and opens out into an arcaded square. Here a pilgrims' hospice, long disappeared, was built in the thirteenth century. What remains from the past is the massive fifteenth-century church of the Ascension, which houses a statue of the Virgin Mary brought here from France in the fourteenth century. Martin and Juan de Landerrain built its marvellous Renaissance belfry. The façade is plateresque, the interior is baroque and the cloister is cool and Gothic.

Pilgrims to the Holy Land also often journeyed to Compostela as well. They brought memories of the church of the Holy Sepulchre, which inspired the design of the octagonal churches at Roncesvalles and Eunate which I had already seen. At my next stop, Torres del Rio, is another, built in the twelfth century. But there is a subtle difference here, seen in the rib-vaulting of its dome. The inspiration of these is Arabic, for Arab architects were so skilful that Christians in Spain frequently turned to them. These vaults of the church of San Sepolcro, Torres del Rio, are directly inspired by those of the chapels of the mosque at Córdoba. Its role for pilgrims was a melancholy one, serving as funeral chapel for those who died on their way.

Viana lies twelve kilometres south-west of Torres del Rio. Sancho VII the Strong founded this fortified spot in 1219 to defend frontier of Navarre. The Estella gate is where pilgrims entered the town, and its whole orientation derives from the pilgrimage route to Compostela. The town is handsome, with coats of arms proudly displayed on some of its patrician houses and an arcaded town hall built in 1688. It boasts a plateresque façade and a couple of towers. What I had not expected was to find the tomb of Cesare Borgia in the imposing fourteenth-century church of Santa Maria — which also boasts a superb Renaissance façade whose sculptures include the labours of Hercules. So used to imagining the Borgias to be Italian, I had no idea till I reached Viana that they were really called Borja and came from Valencia in Spain. Cesare, a cardinal of the Catholic church at the tender age of seventeen, married a sister of the King of Navarre in 1499. As general of the royal army of Navarre he was slain beseiging rebellious Viana in 1507. The citizens of Viana are proud of him, and have put up his statue in the plaza del Sor Simona.

All these are little towns, and Logroño which I next reached seemed ridiculously large. Its towers beckon. I crossed the River Ebro and made for the church of San Bartolomé, whose Romanesque porch is as emaciated as some of the saints sculpted on it. The architecture of its tower is technically described as Mudéjar, a word which was initially used to describe a Muslim living in the lands reconquered by the Christians. Many of these served as architects of Christian churches, to which they brought the horseshoe arches, the stucco work, the elegantly cased and coloured ceilings of their own mosques. Mudéjar architects also relished using brick and ceramics to pattern their buildings, as they did with the tower of San Bartolomé, Logroño.

This Moorish element, which has occurred before, needs little explanation. Hilaire Belloc considered that the two main facts of all Spanish history were, 'First, the Mohammedan tide, swirling up to and over the Pyrenees, next the long ebb thereof which will always be known as the Re-conquista wherein the true Middle Ages were born: wherein the Gothic and the Universities and the vernacular epics and the chivalric spirit welled up for the remaking of Europe.' He added that, 'There is not a town from the edges of Navarre to the extreme South which has not seen the advent, the presence and the retirement of Mohammedan administration, which has not heard the sing-song of the Koran in its schools and heard that echo die out.'

Tumultous clanging bells drew me to the cathedral of Santa Maria la Redonda, whose baroque towers dominate this quarter of the city. The bells were ringing for Mass, and during the service I was able to admire the delightful carved Renaissance stalls and a splendid baroque reredos of 1762, the latter depicting the crucified Jesus on a tree of Jesse and incorporating a fifteenth-century statue of his mother. Exquisitely dressed children carried twigs decorated with baubles, bows and what seemed like lollipops, for this was Palm Sunday, the day when Christians remember the entry of Jesus into Jerusalem, welcomed by fickle disciples waving plam branches. At Logroño some children carried real palm branches, and a little girl read one of the lessons. But I was impatient to see the church of Santiago el Real. The bells of the cathedral rang again to indicate that Mass was finishing, and two ladies who emerged told me that if I crossed the plaza de la Constitución to the west of the cathedral, took an instant turn right and then the second left I should immediately see its tower. I walked up the narrow street leading to the baroque west end, on which Santiago Matamoros, sculpted by Juan de Roan in 1662, triumphantly rides a spirited and virile stallion, a standard in his left hand, his sword raised aloft. Below him are the decapitated heads of four Muslims, caricatured as Negroes. Below them is a statue of Jesus, the Prince of Peace.

The church itself belies all this violence inside – a spacious Gothic building of just one aisle, with a classical reredos occupying the whole eastern wall. I decided to take a drink in a roughish café where the music blared and every single man (for no women were present) either whistled or sang in tune to it. They were talking about a bullfight held to raise money for the restoration of the bullring. And as I left the café I had the good fortune to encounter a Palm Sunday procession, symbolizing the entry of Jesus into Jerusalem.

Two men in blue masks led the procession, their breasts embroidered with a Maltese cross surrounded by four smaller crosses. Their headdresses resembled Arab turbans. Following them were men and children resplendent in green robes and white cloaks. All wore white gloves, and the children carried huge palm leaves. Next came a confraternity bearing a banner embroidered with the flails with which Jesus was beaten before his crucifixion. Its members wore red robes, flails embroidered on the badge on their arms, and as they processed they rhythmically beat drums, the largest drums bringing up the rear. Masked marshals shepherded this part of the procession, their veils terminating in vast pointed hats. The drumming rose to a crescendo of tightly controlled din. A confraternity dressed in black followed them, their emblem a sacred heart on a little white cloak worn over their sombre dress. Next came the purple-clad confraternity of Jesus of Nazareth, men, women, girls and boys playing drums and bugles. Masked men and children in white and blue robes followed them, carrying drums and palm leaves. This group preceded a massive bier on which was a statue of Jesus riding into Jerusalem on his donkey, the Saviour also carrying a palm leaf. The heavy bier was carried by a host of masked men, who stopped frequently to ease their burden. As they marched a leader beat their pace on the bier with a hammer, while they rhythmically hit the ground with their staffs. A host of layfolk followed.

Any pilgrim to Santiago de Compostela should make a brief excursion south, as I did, from Logroño to Clavijo. This is the site of the famous battle of 844 when St James the Great appeared each day to slay the Moors. Till that year the Christians (as the tale has it) were obliged to pay the Muslims an annual tribute of one hundred maidens. King Ramiro I refused, and the Saracen leader Abderramán II went to war against him. With the aid of St James the Moor slayer he was defeated. The plain where the battle took place is dominated by the ruins of a tenth-century castle, set on a spur of rock.

From here I drove on to Navarrete, just south of the N120, a town on a hillside which still preserves the ruins of a twelfth-century pilgrims' hospice founded by the Hospitallers of St John of Acre. All that remains of it is a doorway beside the cemetery. A statue of Santiago Matamoros appears in a niche near the Santiago gate by which you enter Navarrete. The monumental sixteenth-century church of the Assumption here is matched by an equally monumental Romanesque gateway as you leave the town, part of it built from stones cannibalized from the ancient hospice and carved with the legend of Roland. Certainly there are French reminiscences every-where at this point on the pilgrimage. The church in the next village, Ventosa, is even dedicated to San Saturnino, who is patron saint of Toulouse.

The earth between Logroño and Nàjera is rich red, with Rioja vineyards climbing up the westward facing slopes. This is still hilly country, and from one of the hills on the left as you drive on to Nàjera (a hill known as the Poyo de Roldán) Roland is said to have spotted the giant Ferragut asleep outside his castle. Seizing a rock, Roland flung it at Ferragut, splitting his skull, and was thus able to free the Christians imprisoned in the castle. Peaceful Nàjera gives no hint today of these ancient struggles, save for the derivation of its name, which is Arabic for 'place amongst the rocks'. Once again I had reached a river-crossing, bridged in the eleventh century so that pil-grims needed no longer wade through the water. I made my way to the finest monument of Nàjera, the monastic church of Santa Maria la Real. It was founded on 12 December 1052 by King Don Garcia Sanchez III el de Nàjera and his wife Doña Estefania, who intended the monks to care for pilgrims on the way to Compostela. The king, so it was said, had spotted a grotto in a rock on this spot, in which he found a statue of the Virgin Mary along with a bell and a lamp. Their church, soon to be run by the Cluniac monks who fostered the pil-grimage to Santiago, was finished within four years. Little remains of it today, for the present building dates from the fifteenth century. The beautiful cloisters are Spanish Renaissance, but above the high altar with its luscious early eighteenth-century reredos reigns a twelfth-century statue of the Virgin Mary, successor to that dis-covered by King Don Garcia.

Built of red sandstone, the church turns out to be a mausoleum, housing some thirty royal tombs. Here are buried the sovereigns of Navarre, Castile and Léon, lying in flamboyant sarcophagi as if defy-ing death itself. In the sixteenth century the covers of the tombs were renewed, as though to spite death yet further. The finest of all is the Romanesque lid of the tomb of Doña Blanca, queen of King Sancho III and grandchild of El Cid himself, who died in childbirth. It depicts her deathbed. Her soul, like a little baby, is received into heaven by two angels. Three courtiers comfort the grief-stricken king. Along-side King Solomon, the Magi and Jesus with his apostles, the wise and foolish virgins put in an appearance, doubtless to reassure the visitor that Doña Blanca, if no virgin, was numbered among the wise. Adjoining the church is a cloister whose tracery, half-Gothic, half-Renaissance in style, is as wild as any I have seen. It was built between 1517 and 1528.

Not far away in Nàjera I came upon the seventeenth-century parish church of Santa Cruz. It was still Palm Sunday, and the church was packed with worshippers, while its doorway was festooned with leafy twigs. Having already attended Mass, I peered inside this baroque church simply to enjoy the sight of its octagonal sandstone pillars.

It was time to drive to Santo Domingo de la Calzada (which means St Dominic of the Roadway). On the way I spotted on the left a notice on the brim of a hill directing me to the Cistercian abbey of Cañas. The signpost was worth obeying. The abbey, dating from the twelfth to the fourteenth centuries, boasts a two-storeyed Gothic apse and a classical stone belfry. Here too is a monastic graveyard. The cloisters are classically beautiful, and there is an extensive, walled monastery garden with a vegetable plot, an orchard and a vineyard. The Cistercians monks at Cañas still produce lovely pottery, but I was short of ready cash and regret that I bought none.

The first sight of my next station, Santo Domingo de la Calzada, is its baroque church tower rising over the houses of an enchanting town. Pedro I the Cruel had it fortified in 1367, and inside the walls are the most delightful little streets and some splendid houses adorned with coats of arms. The saint who gave this spot its name spent most of his time building roads for the pilgrims and spanning the river with a twenty-four-arched bridge. Rejected by the Benedictines as too stupid to be a monk, Santo Domingo had intended to live alone as a hermit beside the Rio Oja, but the roads he built brought pilgrims to the door of his cell and in 1044 the kindly saint felt obliged to build them a hospice. He was also responsible for one of the most entertaining miracles imaginable. Around his hospice grew the town which bears his name. My intention had been to stay in the very same hospice which Santo Domingo founded, for, rebuilt in the fourteenth century, it has been turned into a state-owned *parador*. Unfortunately it was closed. In the same square rises the Gothic cathedral of the town, which was begun in the first decade of the twelfth century and finished a hundred years later.

Just inside the neo-classical doorway which was added to the cathedral in 1769 is the sepulchre of Santo Domingo. His tomb is physically in the crypt, but a hole has been cut in the pavement of the cathedral so that the tomb can carry a suitably pious statue of the white-bearded saint. Its alabaster canopy is extremely elaborate, the fifteenth-century work of Juan de Rasines and Felipe Bigarny (Philip of Burgundy), and depicts the saint busy with good works, helping up a fallen man, building his bridge and so on. And as a reminder of the most bizarre miracle of the whole pilgrim route, a silver cock and a silver hen are pecking around Santo Domingo's feet.

The story goes that in the late thirteenth or early fourteenth century three distinguished Germans, Archbishop Santis of Cologne, his wife (though how he could have a wife in the Middle Ages I do not know) and their eighteen-year-old son Hugonell, came through here on their way to Compostela. That evening the daughter of the innkeeper where they were lodging made amorous advances to Hugonell, which he resisted. Enraged at the rebuff, the girl took her revenge by hiding a silver goblet in his pilgrim's bag. The next morning she accused Hugonell of stealing it. The town magistrate believed the girl and hanged Hugonell. Distraught, his parents journeyed on to Compostela. On their return they were about to ask for their son's corpse, when they heard the voice of Santo Domingo saying that even though the young man was still hanging from the gibbet, Domingo had kept Hugonell alive because of his innocence. Amazed, the parents rushed to tell the magistrate the news. The latter, who was just about to tuck into a roasted cock and hen, sarcastically responded, 'If that's true, this cock and hen will fly off the dish and start crowing'; which is precisely what they did. So the saying grew up:

> Santo Domingo de la Calzada
> Que canto la gallina después de asada
> (Santo Domingo del la Calzada
> where the roasted hen sang).

In my view the miracle has a most unhappy ending, for opposite Santo Domingo's sepulchre is a bizarre Gothic hencoop, beautifully decorated. Alas, since it was built it has cooped up a succession of miserble cocks and equally miserable hens, who sadly flap around and occasionally croak.

The cathedral of Santo Domingo de la Calzada is full of other treasures, and I spent a long time there. In the crypt I could have wished that the illumination of the saint's Romanesque tomb (which you work with a coin) lasted longer. I climbed back into the main church for an exceedingly rewarding walk around its chapels. This cathedral is a mixture of all sorts of styles which manages somehow to remain a harmonious whole. Its apse is Romanesque, while the three aisles bear pleasingly simple Gothic arches. By contrast the choir is plateresque, with beautiful and elaborate stalls made by Andrés de Nàjera.

In a chapel on the south side I came upon the skull and femur of a newly canonized saint. St Jeronimo Hermosilla was born at Santo Domingo de la Calzada on 30 September 1800. He became a Franciscan monk and missionary and was murdered at Tonkin on 1 November 1861. Long cherished here, Jeronimo Hermosilla was canonized on 19 June 1988. An enthralling and less grisly sight is the retable chapel opposite the door by which I came in, an example of that superabundant baroque style which the Spanish call churrigueresque. The mighty reredos dates from the mid-sixteenth century, the work of Damián Forment. Usually one is shy of going up to the high altar of a church (and often this is forbidden), but there was no one else inside the cathedral Santo Domingo de la Calzada that afternoon, so I dared to go close enough to examine the altar properly and am glad I did so. The west side of the altar is filled with scenes from the Old and New Testaments, beginning with God creating the world out of chaos. Adam and Eve are shown in the garden of Eden, Adam wearing underclothing even though both are still in the age of innocence. Other Old Testament scenes include the Tower of Babel, a naked and drunken Noah, and Jonah being thrown overboard by his exasperated shipmates. The middle of this side of the altar depicts Jesus surrounded by his four evengelists. New Testament episodes include John the Baptist baptizing Jesus, Jesus's pregnant mother going to visit her pregnant cousin, and three disciples asleep while Jesus is praying in the garden of Gethsemane. Every scene is animated, quaint and charming. The reverse of the altar is quite different, silver and plateresque, with Santo Domingo appearing again along with the cock and hen.

St Francis of Assisi is said to have made a pilgrimage to Compostela, and although he never did, the Franciscans flourished here and fostered the tale. Santo Domingo de la Calzada boasts a lovely Franciscan church, rebuilt in 1571 by Juan de Herrera. And beside the *parador* is the little church of Nuestra Señora de la Plaza. Its modern reredos depicts (as one might expect) Santo Domingo de la Calzada with his two birds, and also Jeronimo Hermosilla, dressed in his Franciscan robes and still not a canonized saint (for he is here called Beata Hermosilla).

Leaving Santo Domingo de la Calzada I spotted a sign for the hermitage of Carrasquede and drove to the spot, to be disappointed that the massive eighteenth-century building is private property, with seats and slides and wings and an old pump in its garden. So I drove on towards Villafranca Montes d'Oca, where I intended to stay overnight. My route took me through the village of Redecilla del Camino, which has preserved its ancient hospice as well as some decent medieval houses. The fourteenth-century church houses a most remarkable Romanesque font, the outside of its basin chiselled to represent the walls of the heavenly Jerusalem. At Belorado both the church of Santa Maria and that of San Pedro turned out to be blessed with sculpted effigies of Santiago, in the one case dressed as a pilgrim and in the other posing as a slayer of the Moors. In Santa Maria too a bas-relief depicts him as Matamoros. The arcaded plaza Mayor of the town almost tempted me to find a bed for the night there, but instead I decided to quit the town, passing the chapel of the hospice of St Lazarus. Then at Tosantos high up on the right I spotted what I took to be a troglodyte church, half-made out of a cave, but the evening was drawing in so I decided not to explore the place.

Villafranca Montes d'Oca, a town once peopled by freemen (or Frenchmen), as a thirteenth- and eighteenth-century church dedicated to St James, inside which is said to be the largest shell-shaped font in Spain. For some reason it was transported here from the Philippines. The church also boasts two statues of its patron saint, one of them transformed into a reliquary and containing what is supposed to be a bit of his skeleton. Behind the church two men were vigorously playing a version of pelota, using flat rackets. Nearby a little fountain spouted away.

I stayed at a rather run-down hotel called El Pájaro, where the bartender doubled as waiter and served me with great courtesy and elegance. I sipped what was called *vino blanco*, save that the wine was golden. In the morning I took breakfast in his bar, accompanied by three drunks whom the barman studiously ignored, even when they broke several glasses. They drifted away, and he told me that they had been drinking Rioja all night. As I left I asked for the card of the hotel, and my waiter-barman was so delighted that he gave me a little case of toothpicks. He also told me that at Villafranca Montes d'Oca I could recognize the pilgrims' hospice, dedicated to San Antonio Abad, by its coat of arms and also by the fact that it was being restored; but I failed to find it.

The road to Burgos from Villafranca Montes d'Oca passes through a hefty forest which, as Aimery Picaud observed, was the haunt of thieves and brigands who preyed on the pilgrims. On the right appears the town of Santovenia, perched on a hill, with its church perched even higher. This is where I turned off the main road to find the hospice and sanctuary of San Juan de Ortega. It is named after a twelfth-century monk who, following the example of Santo Domingo, constructed decent roads for the pilgrims to Compostela. I walked around the twelfth-century apse of the Romanesque church, peered down on by medieval carved faces. Then I admired its delicately fluted Gothic porch. This church is dedicated to St Jerome, its Gothic arches rising from a Romanesque crypt. In the right transept is a classical reredos depicting the patron saint engaged in his customary activities, such as beating himself with a rock, being assaulted by demons and removing a thorn from a lion's paw. One pillar of this church is sculpted with knights in armour. Another, carved by an unknown Romanesque virtuoso, depicts not only the Annunciation but also Mary's visit to her cousin Elizabeth, the birth of her son and angels announcing it to the shepherds. The scene of the Nativity is touching: Mary lies in bed, a couple of humble beasts peer over the cradle where Jesus lies in his swaddling clothes, and a star above them glows to guide the kings of the east to the place of his birth. The apse remains pure Romanesque, with wonderful little windows. One of its retables depicts the resurrection of the dead, naked bodies rising to heaven, where Mary and the infant Jesus await them, while the damned lament below.

There is a rare Romanesque font in this church, round and very plain. And in the centre of the building is an elaborate Gothic tomb, which I discovered later was made in 1464 to house the earthly remains of St Juan de Ortega.

I was wondering how to get inside the rest of the sanctuary, when three youths drove up fast in their sports car and told me there was a guided tour. They found the custodian's office, and instantly he stamped my notebook with the official seal of the sanctuary. 'Spaniards, Frenchmen and Germans stay here,' he exclaimed, 'but so far no British, though I know you British have a confraternity of Santiago de Compostela.' Then he took us round the buildings, smoking a cigar except inside the church. We followed him into a tiny pink sandstone cloister and loggia, from which a door opens into the church. The custodian vouchsafed the amazing information that at the spring and autumn equinoxes (21 March and 22 September) at five o'clock in the afternoon a shaft of sunlight falls upon the capital of the Annunciation. Next we visit the wooden-roofed former refectory of the sanctuary, the little pulpit still intact from which someone would read holy books while the rest ate. The custodian explained that the sanctuary had lost its monks in 1864 and fallen into disrepair. Only since 1964 had the decision been made to restore it. Restoration, so far as I could see, had temporarily stopped, for a builder's crane lay idle on rusty tracks. The sacristy was still in terrible shape, its furniture under plastic sheets and the most valuable medieval Mass and music books lying around, along with sections of a dismembered organ-case. We passed through a half-restored and sizeable classical cloister into a room filled with tableaux of John the Baptist, the finest of around 1540 showing Salome with his head. Here too stood a classical retable, presumably meant for the church, on which was depicted St Jerome in his cardinal's hat talking to his lion.

Dormitories with bunk-beds lead off from the cloisters of the sanctuary. Said the custodian, 'We take people in, and they pay what they can.' A notice about payment, written in English and posted on a dormitory door, confirmed this. 'If you can't, God bless you, your remembering and thankfulness will be enough. We wish you on your way to Compostela to be lit by San Juan de Ortega and Santiago.' The last word of the custodian to me was the first he had spoken in my own tongue: 'Goodbye.'

I drove on to Burgos, which stands on a plateau 900 metres above sea-level. Burgos was founded in 884 by the Count of Castile, acting on behalf of King Alfonso III of Léon, as a bulwark against the advancing Moors. The counts decided to live here, and under their rule the city prospered, expanding still more when the kings of Castile and Léon decided to make it their home. Here in 1026 was born one of the most famous heroes of Spain, the mercenary Roderigo Diaz de Vivar, whom the Moors dubbed *Sidi* (which means Lord), a name that gave him his Spanish title El Cid. Eleven years later King Fernando I united under his own rule the kingdoms of Galicia, Castile and Léon, and made Burgos its capital. Only when the monarchy moved its chief home to Valladolid at the end of the fifteenth century did Burgos begin to decline. Even so, some of its citizens were bold enough to revolt against the regime of the Holy Roman Emperor Charles V. He exacted a penance, forcing Burgos to build a superb gateway, the Arco de Santa Maria, where St Mary's bridge crosses the river into the city. It was finished in 1552. The gateway incorporates parts of an eleventh-century gate. A statue of Charles V, his prominent Habsburg jaw well in evidence, stands in the middle of its façade, surrounded by statues of the five medievel patron saints of Burgos with the Blessed Virgin Mary above them.

Scarcely had I entered the city when a sign directed me off to the right to reach the church of San Lesmes. Lesmes was a Frenchman who came here to dig canals and generally sweeten the pilgrims' route to Compostela. At first sight the most remarkable aspect of this dour part-Romanesque, part-Gothic church is its elongated belfry. Then you see that it also boasts on the south side a sweet Gothic porch, which overlooks the plaza de San Juan Evangelista. The plaza houses an equestrian statue and what was once the pilgrims' hospice of St John the Evengelist.

I retraced my steps to the riverside and drove along the Rio Arlanzón to turn right through the Arco de Santa Maria and park near the cathedral. An Englishman laid its foundation stone in 1221, for Bishop Mauricius of Burgos came from my own land. He was assisted by King Ferdinand III, and as the centuries passed the French, the Flemish and the Germans came to Burgos to help construct this magnificent building. Chief amongst these architects was

Hans of Cologne, who designed the west towers in the mid-fifteenth century. The outrageously spiky, octagonal central tower was finished by a Spaniard, Juan de Vallejo, in 1567.

After so many Romanesque buildings in this part of Spain a splendid Gothic one comes as a surprise. In the first chapel on the right as you enter is a gruesome statue of the dying Jesus. Around this thirteenth-century crucifix (known as the *Santissimo Cristo*) grew many legends: that each Friday its carved wounds bled real blood; that it was a direct copy of the dying body of Jesus; that it was covered with human skin. Fair enough it is decked out with real hair, but it was almost certainly carved in the fourteenth century. When I saw it last on that April day in Holy Week, the figure was also dressed in a purple skirt, and many people were kneeling in rapt prayer before it.

At the end of the same aisle is the chapel of Santiago. Its grille depicts St James on a charger, a dying Moor at his feet. This is not the most glamorous of the chapels of this cathedral, for that praise must be reserved for the chapel of the Constables of Castile, with its exquisite sixteenth-century marble tombs of Pedro Fernández de Velasco and Mencia de Mendoza. To the left of them, seemingly perched in a wall-cabinet, a statue of a dying bishop is being pushed into a far too small coffin. The choir stalls are almost as glamorous as this chapel. Boxwood marquetry set in burnished walnut illustrates tales from the Holy Sciptures or the lives of the saints. And above the crossing rises the octagon which I had already admired from outside, supported by four powerful pillars and decorated in the plateresque style so that it resembles lace rather than stonework. In view of my quest for Santiago it also seemed to me right to seek out the pilgrims' gate, which is the north portal of the north transept. Bishop Juan de Fonseca who paid for it appears in the tympanum, kneeling in front of the Virgin Mary, while St James with a scallop shell is sculpted on the right-hand side of the door. Bishop Fonseca may here appear in humble guise, but in 1519 he was also responsible for commissioning Diego de Siloé to build for his cathedral the *Escalera Dorada*, an elaborate double staircase, its gilded railings patterned with medallions and grotesque faces, which only the emperor and such notables as Fonseca himself were allowed to use.

The rain had stopped as I left the cathedral and I was thus able to admire its splendid porches. Who decided that the angels perched in the arcade of the Voroneria doorway should have such sweet little legs? In the delicate sculptures of the Sacramental doorway St James takes a back seat, so to speak, amongst the row of apostles.

Burgos is above all the city of El Cid, and although I was really in pursuit of Santiago de Compostela, from here I decided to walk up to the citadel of the legendary mercenary, by way of the Moorish, horseshoe-arched gateway of San Estéban. Halfway up to the citadel the road offers a superb panorama over the cathedral and virtually over the whole city. On the way you pass the fortress-like church of San Estéban, which now serves as the diocesan museum. Over its mutilated Romanesque portico you can still make out St Stephen, gazing up to Jesus, who reigns in glory in heaven. This particular gaze cost St Stephen his life. The first Christian martyr had already offended the leaders of the Jews by attacking them for failing to listen to and obey the prophets. 'Now when they heard these things, they were enraged, and they ground their teeth against him,' the Acts of the Apostles records. 'But he, full of the Holy Spirit, gazed into heaven and saw the glory of God, and Jesus standing at the right hand of God; and he said, "Behold, I see the heavens opened, and the Son of man standing at the right hand of God." But they stopped their ears and rushed together upon him. And they cast him out of the city and stoned him. . . . And he knelt down and cried with a loud voice, "Lord, do not hold this sin against them." And when he had said this, he fell asleep.'

Then I reached the so-called Solar of El Cid, which encloses a second fortress in its outside walls. I walked back to my car and returned to the pursuit of St James the Great. As you leave Burgos the last major buildings you come across are the Hospice de la Rey and the Convent of Las Huelgas. They form part of what seems like a little village on its own, quite separate from the busy city, with a curved row of houses and a cobbled street and plane trees. King Alfonso VIII founded the Hospice del Rey towards the end of the twelfth century, and Emperor Charles v rebuilt it. St James appears here no fewer than three times and in three distinct guises. Over the gateway he is his biblical self, apostle and missionary, sitting meditating over holy writ (presumably his own epistle). Go through the arch, turn left, and over the plateresque portico of the hospice he has been transformed into the Moor-slayer, a couple of severed Moorish heads at the feet of his steed. Beyond this portico are the superbly carved Renaissance doors of the hospice chapel. They depict a group of pilgrims, among them an entire family, on the road to Compostela, many with cockle-shells, gourds and staffs. The procession is led by St Michael, as usual slaying a dragon, and by the Holy Roman Emperor himself. As she walks a mother demurely suckles her child. Her husband looks back to urge on their weary son. All three are wearing sturdy boots. Beside them is an almost naked, emaciated and shoeless beggar. He is being comforted by the pilgrim saint himself.

The Convent of Las Huelgas began life as a royal holiday retreat.

In 1175 King Alfonso VIII transformed it into a Cistercian monastery, to be inhabited by a hundred women of noble birth. Work was begun on building a concent chapel in 1180. The square, fortified belfry of the church, with its round staircase tower, is still Romanesque, as is the extremely beautiful smaller cloister, with its twin pillars gleaming a brilliant white in the sun on the day I saw them.

In the early Gothic chapel are buried, along with the founder and his English wife Eleanor in their twin tombs, another fifty or so members of the royal family of Léon, in tombs which depict lions and castles. The finest sepulchre, I think, is that of Princess Blanca of Portugal, held up by a couple of mild Romanesque lions. This chapel boasts five churrigueresque altars, and one chapel in the Mujédar style, dedicated to Santiago. Over its baroque altar sits a strange late thirteenth-century statue of the saint. He carries a sword, presumably a reference to that which decapitated him (according to the Acts of the Apostles, chapter 12, verse 2). His arms are jointed, and with this sword were knighted members of the Order of Santiago. They would cry *Santiago y cierra España* ('St James, and close ranks against the enemy'), so it is perhaps fitting that the convent museum displays the red standard which Alfonso VIII captured from the tent of the Saracen leader at the battle of Las Navas de Tolosa. Here in the late fifteenth century, a local guide-book told me, a German pilgrim named Hermann Kunig de Vach discovered a plaque marking the spot where the prior of the hospice had been shot through with arrows after it was discovered that he had deliberately poisoned a hundred other pilgrims to Compostela. There is no sign of the plaque today; but the guide-book also revealed that Hermann Kunig de Vach came from Strasbourg, and in Strasbourg cathedral, as I remember, is a magical sixteenth-century altar triptych, glistening in gold leaf, one of whose carved saints has a cockle-shell pinned to his hat and wears sturdy boots.

Today the environs of the convent are more homely. I walked through a fortified gateway to the west of the convent to discover a dolphin fountain and a medieval pilgrims' cross. Christ is crucified on one side; on the other are the Madonna and Child. Whoever inhabits the house on top of the defensive gateway was hanging washing fom a clothes-line stretching below the windows.

CHAPTER FIVE

FROM BURGOS TO THE CITY OF ST ISIDORE

BURGOS – SASAMÓN – CASTROJERIZ – BOADILLA DEL CAMINO – FRÓMISTA – VILLACÁZAR DE SIRGA – CARRIÓN DE LOS CONDES – SAHAGÚN – SAN PEDRO DE LA DUEÑAS – GRAJAL DE CAMPOS – MANSILLA DE LAS MULAS – SAN MIGUEL DE ESCALADA – LÉON.

THE TERRAIN running north-west from Burgos towards Las Quintanillas begins with low, eroded limestone hills and then transforms itself into green hilly fields. The road next runs up and down hill again through uncultivable lands and then rises on a flat and exceedingly stony plain. I was looking for the signs to Sasamón, which lies north of the road. Its ruined castle seems to have stepped out of a medieval manuscript. This spot was the seat of a bishopric in the Middle Ages. Some of the medieval walls are still intact, and the thirteenth-century church of Santa Maria la Real is decorated with a superbly sculpted portal whose tympanum portrays Christ in majesty, waited on by the four evangelists and the twelve apostles. That Sasamón also lay on the medieval pilgrim route is confirmed by its plateresque retable, dedicated to Santiago himself.

Returning south-west through the quaintly stepped plateau or *mesa*, at Villasardino, where the river is crossed by a thirteenth-century bridge, I turned south for Castrojeriz, the 'Castum Sigerci' founded by a Goth named Sigeric in 760. A ruined castle dominates a mound here and allows the dusty brown town to live up to its name, but its most celebrated monument is the church of Nuestra Señora de Manzano, which means Our Lady of the Apple-tree. Founded for the Cistercians in 1214 by Doña Berenguera, the church still shelters a medieval statue of this particular Virgin Mary, still retaining its thirteenth-century colours. Amongst the many other treasures in this church (for it has been deconsecrated and become an art museum) is a curious painting of a pilgrim bound for Santiago. Castrojeriz also boasts a second fine church, the Renaissance Santo Domingo. San Juan is a third massive church in this small town, Gothicized in the fourteenth century but retaining a charming twelfth-century cloister. One of my guide-books declares that a skeleton surrounded by cockle-shells was discovered when the town was repaving its plaza Mayor, and turned out to be carrying fourteenth-century English and French coins.

I wound my way westwards towards Frómista. The route passes through Itero del Castillo, where the River Pisuergo is crossed by a beautiful twelfth-century bridge with eleven regular round arches. At the next hamlet, Itera de la Vega, pilgrims would call at the hermit-age of La Pidead, to kneel before its statue of Santiago in his own pil-grim's dress, before reaching Boadilla del Camino and pausing once again in the Gothic church of Santa Maria, which is famous most of all for a beautifully sculpted Gothic pillar.

The church of San Martin at Frómista is one of the most harmo-nious Romanesque buildings I had yet encountered, and one of the oldest in Spain. Two symmetrical round towers flank its west façade. Over the apse a simple octagonal lantern rises to a shallow, pointed roof of tiles. Carved on the church are, I calculate, over three hundred corbels, and the exterior of the apse is delicately patterned. This hori-zontal chequerboard decoration became a hallmark of Romanesque churches on the pilgrimage routes to Santiago. Built for Benedictine monks in 1066 at the expense of the widow of King Sancho the Great of Navarre, San Martin is all that remains of a monastery which was later taken over by the Cistercians and offered hospitality to count-less pilgrims. At Frómista pilgrims could also stay in a sixteenth-century hospice, the Hospital de Palmeros, which has been turned into a modern hotel. In the plaza Mayor on which it stands is a modern statue of the patron saint of sailors, St Telmo. Born here in 1190, he balances precariously in a tiny coracle with a huge anchor, set on a plinth rising from a little pool. Further on in the town rise the Gothic church of San Pedro with its Renaissance retable, and the flamboyant Gothic church of Santa Maria del Castillo, which boasts a yet more monumental sixteenth-century retable housing twenty-nine statues.

I left the town by way of calle General Mola, which passes the former hermitage of Santiago, and soon reached Villacázar de Sirga. This is a ramshackle enough village, but it is blessed with a superb church, the thirteenth-century Gothic Santa Maria la Blanca, with a chapel dedicated to the pilgrim St James. This massive building once belonged to a hospice run by the Knights Templar. When it was being built, in 1196, the Muslims (so runs the story related in the medieval songs of the epic poet King Alfonso x the Wise) were massing to des-troy it when they were repulsed solely by the power of a white stone statue of the Blessed Virgin Mary. This is the Santa Maria la Blanca from which the church derives its name. Alfonso's *Cantigas* also relate how this statue was reputed to heal sick pilgrims who knelt before her, as well as saving sailors from storms and tempests. Today the church houses a tomb of Alfonso's brother, Don Felipe, and his second bride Doña Leonor. Don Felipe, having sat at the feet of the celebrated Thomas Aquinas in Paris, was ordained priest and eventually consecrated Archbishop of Seville. But when his brother Alfonso rejected the hand of his fiancée Christine of Norway, Felipe took her side in the quarrel and went so far as to renounce his orders in order to marry her. After her death he married another, Leonor, and she it is who lies beside him here today, both of them sculpted lying on top of their tomb.

Seven kilometres further on I reached a spot steeped in Spanish legend – Carrión de los Condes. According to the story of El Cid, the Count of Carrión married his daughters simply to obtain their dowries, and then behaved abominably to them until El Cid took his revenge, sending his knights to slaughter the Count. The daughters then married other nobles and lived happily ever after. The town, with its medieval walls, is the first sizeable spot after Burgos, and the first sight as I entered was the sixteenth- to eighteenth-century convent church of Santa Clara, set on a hill. Inside, Our Lady is the centre of a huge classical retable which stands oddly offset in the Gothic apse. When I arrived, one man and seventeen women were being led through the Rosary by a priest, and the apse seemed to be leaning perilously, so I withdrew quietly and speedily. I found the twelfth-century church of Santa Maria del Camino and the Hospice de la Herrada. Among the carvings on the porch of the church are a couple of bull heads – a possible reference to the tale that annually at Carrión de los Condes one hundred Christian maidens were sacrificed by the Moors, who let wild bulls loose upon them. Inside are some wild churrigueresque retables.

But the glory of this tortuous little town is the façade of the church of Santiago, facing on to a narrow street of medieval houses. At the centre of its frieze Jesus sits enthroned amongst the evangelists, with rows of apostles spread out on either side. Though the pattern and conception is Romanesque, the faces and the tortuous dress of the figures already presage the elegance of the Gothic. Beneath the frieze is a strip of chequerboard decoration. Alas, of the twelve sculpted apostles, only seven retain their heads. On the porch are musicians and medieval craftsmen, one blowing a pair of bellows, while in another scene knights joust.

By way of an eleventh-century pilgrims' bridge I crossed the

River Carrión and passed the plateresque cloisters, with their ornate medallions and busts, all (save the church) that remain from the former monastery of San Zoilo. These cloisters were built by Juan de Badagaz in the late sixteenth century. As for St Zoilo, he was a martyr slaughtered at Códoba during the Roman persecutions of the early church. His precious relics were brought here shortly after the monastery had been founded in the eleventh century by Teresa, the wife of Count Gómez Díaz. The monastery church today is mostly baroque in style, but her medieval tomb still stands in its Capilla Mayor.

The province of Palencia has set up carved stones marked with scallop shells beside the N120, giving details of the churches in the villages alongside the route, so I was continually tempted to turn off and visit them. At Calzada de las Molinos a couple of storks were nesting on a church dedicated to Santiago. Quintanilla de la Cueza boasts a sixteenth-century church and beyond it a Roman villa. The road from Carrión de los Condes to Sahagún passes through refreshing, often treeless and cultivated countryside. Along it the villages bear names redolent of the pilgrim route, such a Terradillos de los Templarios and San Nicolás del Real Camino.

I have several times found myself in Sahagún, and once had the good fortune to arrive there in time for the Saturday market. It sets itself up in and around the main square with its wooden arcades. Wicker baskets, fans, little corn dollies and children's toys are on sale, as well a modern cassettes from which music continually blares (sometimes the latest popular star, sometimes traditional Castilian music). Huge pears and cauliflowers, kitchen ware and ceramics, watches and fruit trees, axes and chisels, bread, biscuits, smoked sausages and walnuts weigh down stalls. A smell of cured ham mingles with the gentler scent of cheeses. I bought myself a couple of leather belts and a pot of honey.

This small town was one one of the most prosperous in Castile, bordered as it is by two rivers and hosting an annual market which lasted for a fortnight. The French, the Moors and the Jews all lived in their own quarters of the town, and the Christians built themselves no fewer than nine churches as well as four hospices for pilgrims. Four of the churches have survived. At the top of the town are two neighbours, the churches of San Trinidad and San Juan, and from the white façade of the latter you can see ahead the tower of San Lorenzo. I strolled down to it along a curving street which was completely empty even though this was market day. Though the apse of this thirteenth-century church is Romanesque, its blind arches are slightly pointed in the Mudéjar fashion, and in the apse is a Moorish horseshoe arch. Pigeons huddled everywhere on its four-tiered, square tower. A Romanesque arcade shaded the south side from the hot sun. The church was locked. Around the corner from the plaza San Lorenzo rises the brick church of San Tirso, the centre one of its three Romanesque apses rising from stone. Different-coloured bricks add patterns to the walls. This time the square tower has three tiers, and I spotted little cockle-shells on the capital of one of the pillars.

San Tirso faces the ruins of the twelfth-century Benedictine abbey of San Binio. Monks had fled here from Córdoba in 904 to escape the depredations of the Arabs. Then King Alfonso VI brought Cluniac monks to Sahagún from France to reform the order, another example of the cross-currents between France and Spain on this pilgrimage route. The stern classical tower of the monastery is intact, standing alongisde a ruined Doric gateway and bearing a cockle-shell on the coat of arms which is carved on it. Plaza San Binio is in better condition, sporting a little fountain. And Benedictine nuns are still here. Through an eighteenth-century archway, monumental on one side while the other looks like the backside of a stage-set, you reach their eighteenth-century church, recognizable chiefly for the modern statue of St Benedict outside it. It was put here in 1980, a thousand years after his death. The church houses the tombs of Alfonso VI, who died in 1109, and his wife Isabella, who was the daughter of Aben Omar, the Emir of Seville.

I walked up a little rise to see the remarkable red-brick sanctuary just outside Sahagún which is dedicated to La Pellegrina, the lady-pilgrim, a reference to an eighteenth-century statue of a woman in pilgrim's clothing inside it. This church, founded by the Franciscans, was in terrible condition, though happily being restored (or at least being made safe, as one of the workmen told me). A nearby mount looks suspiciously like a former hill-fort, though today its underground house with a chimney poking out of the top of the mound cares for the tools of the workmen perched precariously on top of the Santuario de la Pellegrina. Climbing to the top of the mound I sat and gazed at the ancient sanctuary. The cusped blind arches towards the west end are decidedly Arabic. The belfry seems about to tumble down. The sanctuary overlooks a long wide plain, and in the distance the peaks of the mountain range were snow-covered.

Where the road bends below the sanctuary of the pilgrim woman a signpost suggests you leave the Camiño de Santiago to drive for four kilometres to visit San Pedro de la Dueñas. I decided to follow the tree-lined route to this village. Four Romanesque lions suppport the fountain in its central square, which is shaded by the long, two-storeyed brick wall of a monastery. A double-storeyed brick belfry rises from the stone apse of its church. I went through the classical porch of the monastery and rang the doorbell, but nobody came. Then I walked around the west end of the building. The gate of the monastery garden was open, so I was able to sniff the roses growing over its pergolas. Here are seats, a well and a statue of Jesus displaying his sacred heart. Beyond it is the doorway where food is dispensed to wayfarers, or so I supposed, since a tray with two empty dishes lay outside a little hatch. As if to discourage persistent beggars, a notice on one wall carried Jesus's warning that man does not live by bread alone, while on another wall we were told that to share Jesus's sufferings enables us to become his brethren. The doormat was more encouraging, bearing one the word *Hola!* (Hello). So I rang the doorbell here too, and once again nobody came.

Fortunately in the square was a hostel called the Plaza Bar. It was filled with men, who had seen me poking around and who now kindly asked me what I had been looking for. When I told them my business one asked if I had seen another remarkable spot nearby named Grajal de Campos. He directed me back to Sahagún, telling me to turn right at the town and look for the sign to Villada. Grajal de Campos is an ancient, irregular village, virtually derelict and quite remarkable. A little bridge crosses the River Valderaducy, beyond which towers a battlemented castle built in the sixteenth century by Fernando de Vega, chief commander of Castile. Massive square bastions rise from each corner. An old cannon pokes out of one of its machicolated walls. I walked into the newly-cobbled main square of the village for another surprise: a huge, tumbledown Romanesque church with an oddly shaped belfry, standing next to a disused, classically arcaded monastery.

Then I drove the five kilometres back to Sahagún, turned left and crossed an ancient bridge to make my way to Léon. Occasionally wooded and gently rolling countryside opens on either side of the thirteen-kilometre stretch of road which leads south-west as far as Gordaliza del Pino. The provinces are gradually improving this stretch of the motor road to Compostela, and the village now lies off it, a little to the south. I turned into it, first of all to explore without prying the remarkable phenomenon of the troglodyte houses. These underground homes built into caves are still inhabited all along this section of the route. The branch road into Gordaliza del Pino runs through a veritable village of these homes, their chimneys poking up through the ground. Naturally the village is equipped, so far as I could see, with all that one needs for twentieth-century life here: donkeys, electricity, dogs, motor cars and a church. I peeped into some of the houses, outside which people were sitting but thought it would be discourteous to ask to see more. The church, further on in the village and standing amongst some more conventional houses, is alas not troglodyte. Built out of brick, it is both Romanesque and Mudéjar.

From this intriguing spot my route continued westwards along the N120, to make a sharp right turn on meeting the N601. This road runs almost directly north-west to Léon. On the way there are two particular treats. The first is the little town of Mansilla de las Mulas, which in the Middle Ages could shelter pilgrims in four separate hospices. When Aimery Picaud passed this way Mansilla was entirely surrounded by fortifications. The eastern gateway still stands, two towers intact, two in ruins. Unfortunately other signs of decline are to be found here, for a thirteenth-century church, once dedicated to St Martin, has become a shop, and the early sixteenth-century Augustinian convent is in ruins, part of its stones built into the local abattoir. That said, the arcaded square boasts houses rising from columns, and the bars are picturesque. The best sight of walls and crenellations is reserved for later, as you leave Mansilla and cross the Rio Esla, pausing to turn back and enjoy the view. The look-out points have defended the town for eight hundred years. Even so, these walls too seem to have virtually had their day.

Just beyond the town in the direction of Léon a signpost directs you to the right towards the monastery of San Miguel de Escalada. The countryside had become flat and inhospitable again. As I drove along the narrow side road, tunnelled rock formations in the cliffs ahead indicated the possibility of more troglodyte homes, while not too far ahead rose a far more awesome mountain range. Reaching a village I began to fear that I should discover a spot as tumbledown as Mansilla de las Mulas. Women were washing clothes at the village well. The older houses of the village were plastered simply with brown mud and a little straw, and newer ones, built out of breeze-blocks, were destined for the same treatment. Nowhere could I find any signs of a monastery, so finally I had to ask a man riding through the village on a bicycle. San Miguel de Escalada lies just beyond the village, round a corner and up the hill, he said.

It is in fact a superb site for a monastery, isolated enough, and here sheltered by the hill from the fierce winds which must sometimes whistle across the flat plain. Surrounded by well-kept green grass, the remains of the monastery, consisting of a double church and a magical arcaded outside gallery, are also in superb condition, constructed of white stone with red-tiled roofs. As I wandered around it, a custodian appeared from his lair to let me in.

This monastery was founded in 913 by monks of Córdoba who

wished to escape the dominance of the Moors, yet it offers one of the finest examples of Mozarabic architecture on the whole pilgrim route, displaying how much these Christians had learned from the architectural techniques of their conquerors. Eleven cusped arches of great delicacy uphold the external gallery, the oldest such in Spain. It shelters Romanesque tombs of abbots and their compatriots and its inside wall is inscribed with their epitaphs.

The custodian told me that their first church was consecrated in 957, the rest being finished around 1150. We went in down steps to three aisles, separated by more exquisite cusped arches rising from marble pillars whose capitals are carved with stylized leaves. Similar arches separate the east end of the church from the rest, forming a kind of Byzantine iconostasis. If anything, I judged the workmanship of the older part of the building yet more delicate than the later.

The monastery of San Miguel de Escalada is now classed as a national monument. The custodian told me that 50,000 people visit it each year, which surprises me enormously for the press of them could scarcely squeeze along the dusty little road and through the nearby village; but when I suggested this, he volunteered the further information that the following day twelve bus-loads of Germans were arriving. I seem to have picked an excellent solitary moment to visit the sanctuary. Finally he told me that a few kilometres further on the Cistercian monks still inhabiting the twelfth-century cloister of Gradefes welcome visitors, but I am sorry to record that I was growing anxious to reach Léon and therefore did not pay them a visit. Then I asked him what I owed him for his kindness, and he asked for some cigarettes. For once I almost regretted not smoking.

Pilgrims would undoubtedly have welcomed the hospitality of the Cistercians of Gradefes, for the scenery from Mansilla de las Mulas to Léon grows more hostile even to this day, and we have abundant records of pilgrims in the past being robbed or murdered on this stretch of their road to Santiago. Léon itself, like a skilful showman, offered them its treasures in ascending order of glamour. The first church they would spot as they reached the outskirts of the city from the west was Santa Ana. When it was owned by the Knights of St John of Jerusalem it was named the church of the Holy Sepulchre and thus reminded visitors of that other great pilgrimage route to Jerusalem. The church lies in what is now a bustling outer suburb of Léon, situated in the arcaded plaza de Santa Ana just north of the avenida de Madrid. This was my route into the city, so I parked and went to look at Santa Ana. Unfortunately it was locked. Over its west doorway is inscribed a Maltese cross, and a stork was nesting on its brick Romnesque belfry.

To evoke a memory of pilgrims of yesteryear I walked from this west doorway towards the heart of the city by taking calle Barahona, which narrows into the cobbled calle de Puerta Moneda. This street starts at the third-century Roman walls of the inner city, for Léon was a Roman encampment and derives its name from the seventh Roman legion, which camped here from around AD 70. Calle de Puerta Moneda is delightfully irregular, and enlivened with elaborate overhanging lamps. The smallest house, which is ancient indeed, bears a notice declaring that 'In this house was born the illustrious politician and vet, D. Felix Gordon Ordas, b.1885, d.1973.' I followed calle de Puerta Moneda into calle de Herreros to discover a church known to generations of pilgrims as Santa María del Camiño and built in the twelfth century. Since then, as you can see from the steps leading down beside its north wall, the ground has risen surprisingly. Beyond its venerable apse is the plaza Santa María del Camiño, a square ancient enough to match it – though no Romanesque architect would possibly have countenanced such charming irregularity. Two huge plane trees shade the square, which is watered (literally when the water runs over the bowls) by a neo-classical fountain set up at the expense of Reynardo Carlos in 1789. I came into the square by the north side of the cathedral, past a medieval house with an overhanging balcony held up on wooden pillars and a Renaissance house whose balcony rests on stone ones. At the opposite corner of the square rises what seem to be the haphazard buildings of a former convent, with a Renaissance door. At the top of its belfry two storks perched amongst their nest of twigs, so I sat on the edge of the fountain, and the storks peered down at me and I stared up at them.

Calle de Herreros next took me to the tiny triangular plaza de la Concepción, in which stands a convent of the Holy Conception founded in the fifteenth century. Its long projecting balcony is decorated with a neatly painted frieze. This is where pilgrims turned into what they called the calle de la Rúa, a medieval street which exists to this day. It leads to plaza San Marcelo and two splendid monuments of Léon. The first is the church dedicated to the city's patron saint, Marcelo. A member of the seventh Roman legion, Marcelo, along with his wife and son, embraced Christianity in the third century, and all chose martyrdom rather than renounce their faith. The present church, though it dates in part from the twelfth century, was substantially rebuilt in the sixteenth to the designs of Baltasár Gutiérrez and Juan de Rivero. Above its high altar is a magnificent reredos, like a multi-layered cream cake. Mass was ending as I went into the church, and the whole ensemble was beautifully lit. As the worshippers left, I walked towards the east end for a better view and

Above A troglodyte church, serving one of the many troglodyte villages just outside Santo Domingo de la Calzada.

Right This elaborate screen in the cathedral of Santo Domingo de la Calzada protects the tomb of Santo Domingo himself, who in the eleventh century cared for pilgrims to Santiago de Compostela by building roads and a hospice.

At Burgos the mid-sixteenth century Arco de Santa Maria was built on the orders of Emperor Charles V, whose own statue is set amongst five saints.

Above Burgos cathedral, one of the finest Gothic buildings in Spain.

Above The Romanesque doorway of the church of Santiago at Carrión de los Condes.

Above The ruined Franciscan monastery of La Pellegrina, on its hill outside Sahagún.

In the triple-lobed arch over the doorway of the pilgrims' hospice at
León, St. James urges on his charger while slaughtering Moors.

Above A pilgrimage cross, and in the distance the twin towers of the cathedral of Astorga.

Right The church of El Cebrero dates from the ninth century.

Below An elegant pair of doors at Villafranca del Bierzo.

Above Although most twentieth century pilgrims follow the modern roads to Santiago de Compostela, in the middle ages men and women journeyed along this ancient route above Triacastela.

Right A massive Benedictine monastery dominates the little village of Samos.

An eighteenth century statue of St. James the Great above one of the
gateways in the walls of Lugo, which were built in the third century AD.

Above The baroque and churrigueresque extravagance of its cathedral towers above the city of Santiago de Compostela.

Right Known as the Puerta de la Platerias (the silversmiths' doorway), this exquisitely carved eleventh century entrance constitutes one of the oldest parts of the cathedral at Santiago de Compostela.

the priest switched off the illumination, leaving only the statue of a sternly resolute Marcelo (carved by Gregorio Fernández) lit up at the centre of the ensemble.

Perhaps the saint is trying not to care that so many nearby buildings are covered with cockle-shells (especially the one immediately opposite the west door), an indication of how Santiago has overtaken the rightful patron of this city. Still, the very existence of the pilgrimage route and the situation of the church of San Marcelo beside the Rúa had brought some of the wealth that paid for such a sumptuous rebuilding. Across the square stands a remarkable late nineteenth-century pile which is a symbol of modern wealth, the Casa de los Botines, which today houses a savings bank – though it was intended as a private house plus apartments to let. It was designed by the Catalan art nouveau architect Antonio Gaudí. Extraordinary though he was, Gaudí did not turn his back on the past as much as some architectural writers have suggested. In particular, he was responsive to the Muslim elements in Spain's legacy. Although by the time he came to build this house at Léon, in the first half of the 1890s, Gothic forms were increasingly preoccupying Gaudí, and the Mudéjar influence is still there. The Casa de los Botines is not my favourite among Gaudí's work, which is to be found in Barcelona. Yet its originality remains startling, with Gaudí's talent at its most distinctive here, I think, in the complex ironwork and the serpentine arches.

Of course few pilgrims over the centuries have come across Gaudí on the road to Compostela, though he puts in a more distinctively religious appearance shortly. Many more will have passed and even visited the nearby Palacio de los Guzmanes. Built for a Bishop of Calahorra, Quiñones and Gusman in 1560, almost certainly to the designs of Roderigo Gil de Hontañon, it encloses an unusually restrained but still plateresque two-storeyed courtyard. In the entrance is a reference to Santiago: a man dressed as a pilgrim washes the feet of another. Is the washing being done by Jesus himself?

This is the finest palace in Léon, but it forms merely a prelude to the glorious stages on the way through the city that pilgrims in the past would encounter before seeking lodgings in the Hospice of San Marcos. I, however, needed to bring my car to my hotel. Before doing so I slaked my thirst on a coffee in one of the many bars crowded into the narrow streets of medieval Léon.

My hotel, the Riosol in avenida de Palencia just south of the Rio Bernesga, was the most upmarket of all those I had yet used. Excellent in almost all respects, it lacked a garage, so I was obliged to drive a few hundred metres into the centre of the city in order to park. Since I was fairly late the garage parking was full, so I parked in the street in front of a cake shop, an action which the following day enabled me to learn something about the character of the Léonese. Léon is a handsome city, with wide avenues as well as narrow cobbled streets, with fountains illuminated in the evening and welcoming bars and restaurants, so that to stroll back to an hotel from a parking place and back again the following morning was no trouble. What upset me was to find a flat tyre when I next reached my car. Inevitably the traveller imagines that some vandal is responsible. I went into the cake shop to borrow a telephone directory, but the smiling, ample lady behind the bar would have none of it. On my behalf she telephoned a garage and summoned help. I bought one of her cream cakes and retired to read a newspaper over a large coffee in a nearby café. When the help arrived, the lady came running across to tell me. Nor would she accept a single peseta for the telephone call.

To find the superb Pilgrims' Hospice of San Marcos I walked back from the cake shop almost as far as the Hotel Riosol, but before crossing the river turned right through a park of neat lawns and huge chestnut trees. Ahead a bridge whose foundations date back to Roman times is presumably the reason why in the mid-twelfth century Queen Doña Sancha set up a church here and a little hospice. The foundation coincided with the development of that most famous of Spanish military-religious orders, the Knights of St James. In 1171, by agreement with the Archbishop of Santiago, these knights were formally placed under the protection of the apostle himself, and their Master was admitted as a canon of his cathedral. Four years later these same knights had gained the approval of Pope Alexander III. He decreed that their spiritual guidance should derive from a council of clergymen, under the direction of a prior, and that the order should live by the Rule of St Augustine. Two other chief officers were now appointed to serve alongside the Master. One of them was the prior of Léon.

The duties of these knights included the protection of pilgrims, including the care of the sick and the Christian burial of those who died on the route. Soon at Léon they were in charge of the hospice and monastery of San Marcos. The order grew immensely rich and, meeting at Valladolid in 1513, its chapter decided on a complete rebuilding of their Léon hospice, its church and its cloister. Chief among the architects charged with the work was the plateresque genius Juan de Badajoz.

By 1549 the façade stretched for some hundred sumptuous metres. Slender-columned windows topped with pilasters vary the long horizontal lines of the decoration. Over the florid central entrance Santiago is sculpted in a triple-lobed Mudéjar arch, urging on his charger and slaying countless Moors. From either side of the arched doorway a row of portrait medallions, representing personages from pagan antiquity as well as from the Old and New Testaments and Christian kings and queens, stretches along the front of the building. They were sculpted by Badajoz and his colleague Juan de Horozco. Some of their juxtapositions are quaint. For instance, the Holy Roman Emperor Charles v appears between busts of Augustus Caesar and Trajan, while Queen Isabella of Castile is flanked by the Jewish heroine Judith and the Roman Lucretia, who was raped by Sextus Tarquinia. The whole remains magnificent, even though many statues have disappeared from their niches, some are mutilated and part of the fantastic cornice is broken. Even Santiago carries a broken sword, and his horse has lost its front legs. Near to the saint a king dresses humbly (though still gorgeously) in brimmed hat, bears a staff and is festooned with scallop shells.

The hospice is today partly a luxury hotel and partly a museum. At the far end from the river is its chapel, and just a hint of the earlier buildings can be spotted on the south side over the plateresque façade. The west front of the chapel itself is not so riotously decorated, simply studded with hundreds of cockle-shells. For some reason it is defended by a fake cannon. Again most of the statues have gone from their niches, but God the Father still appears, as well as an intact Deposition from the Cross on the left.

Pediments and bosses hang from the vaulting inside the church, decoration which makes all the greater an impact by rising from virtually bare walls. In case the cockle-shells on the west wall have not sufficiently impressed the visitor, a massive gallery is studded with more of them. The canons and knights of St James ministered suitably to their sense of their own importance by commissioning double-tiered and richly carved stalls for themselves, sculpted by the Renaissance masters Juan de Juni, Guillen Doncel and Pedro de Salamanca. This church is today but the prelude to the museum of religious art and archaeology. Apart from the interest of its contents, a visit is worthwhile simply to gaze on the overwrought baroque ceiling of the sacristy. The chapter house boasts another elaborate – and quite different – ceiling. I have to report, however, that when I visited the hospice the formal garden of box-hedged beds in the middle of its cloister was overgrown.

In the square facing this hospice has been set up a fifteenth-century cross which once guided pilgrims over the pass of Portillo. Sculpted on it are scenes from the Gospels and also St Raphael dressed in pilgrim's costume. Further north I could make out already the twin baroque towers of the church of San Juan y San Pedro de

Reneuva, and I trust no one will in times to come obscure the view by building too high on the waste land as you approach the church. It has a fine baroque façade, but I wanted to reach the Real Basilica of San Isidoro and did not stay long. At the top of calle de Renueva I turned right along avenida Ramon y Cajal alongside part of the ancient city walls, which the Muslim El Mansour demolished at the end of the tenth century and the people of Léon put up again in the next. The bastions rest on rock-like slabs developing into irregular stones and slates as they rise. Rising over the wall at the far end is the Romanesque tower of San Isidoro, known from the clock on its weathervane as the Torre del Gallo.

On first thoughts Isidore is a strange saint to have such a royal basilica dedicated to him at Léon, for he was a distinguished arch-bishop not of this city but of Seville, in which see he had succeeded his brother around 600. In 610 at a council held at Toledo, the bishops agreed to acknowledge him as Primate of all Spain. A prolific founder of monasteries and a redoubtable missionary, Isidore also poured out a remarkable number of treaties – on scientific and historical matters as well as on religion. He died in 635, having completed his last work which was destined to be the favourite encyclopedia of the Middle Ages, published again and again and endlessly perused for informa-tion about mathematics and medicine, grammar and rhetoric, history and theology. Isidore presided over great councils of the Spanish church, and fourteen years after his death another council described him as 'the excellent doctor, the late ornament of the Catholic church, the most learned man, given to enlighten the latter ages, always to be named with reverence.' Dante's *Paradiso* pictured his ardent spirit gleaming in heaven.

No one doubted his charity, sanctity and sacrificial manner of life, and tales of the extraordinary fervour of his life soon prolifer-ated. The eighteenth-century hagiographer Alban Butler described the manner of his death thus:

> Perceiving his end to draw near, he entreated two bishops to come to see him. With them he went to church, where one of them covered him with sackcloth and the other put ashes on his head. Clothed with the habit of penance, he stretched his hands towards heaven, prayed with great eagerness, and begged aloud the pardon of his sins.

Having received the Last Sacrament, Butler continues, Isidore 're-mitted the bonds of all his debtors, exhorted the people to charity, and caused all the money which he had not yet disposed of to be distributed among the poor.'

St Isidore was buried inside Toledo cathedral, flanked by his brother St Leander (who had been his predecessor as archbishop) and his sister St Florentina. His bones reached Léon as part of the same cult of relics which had brought about the alleged discovery of the bones of St James at Compostela and also because of the power of the Moors which Santiago helped to combat. In the mid-eleventh century, with the Moors ruling Seville, the envoys of King Ferdinand I of Castile and Léon managed to persuade the Emir of Seville to sell him Isidore's relics. The basilica which now houses these bones stands on the site of an ancient church which was dedicated to St John the Baptist. At the end of the tenth century El Mansour had demolished it, but under the patronage of King Alfonso v it had been rebuilt. This church was deemed far too humble for the corpse of Isidore, which reached Léon in 1063, and Ferdinand I and his successors set about replacing it with the superb basilica I had just reached.

To walk to San Isidoro after visiting San Marcos is to plunge back three hundred years from the plateresque to the Romanesque. Around the corner from the south-west tower are two Romanesque entrances. Above the first one, which bears a sculpted frieze of the signs of the zodiac, is a massive equestrian statue of St Isidore, added in the eighteenth century. Comparing how the eighteenth century envisaged Isidore with the Romanesque archbishop who is carved on the left of the doorway, I prefer the latter. A quaint beast (one of his pets, perhaps) peers around his waist. The right-hand doorway is far simpler and to my mind more satisfying. Its tympanum depicts the deposition of Jesus from the cross. A man with huge pincers is pulling a nail out of the left hand of the dead Jesus, while the Virgin Mary kisses his utterly dead right hand. The scene is flanked by a simple carved relief of St Paul.

This doorway is known as the porch of pardon. Just as I was about to enter it, a stork flapped its way through the sky and landed on one of the elegant pediments on the right. The Romanesque pillars inside the basilica bear lovely carved capitals. The transept is yet more elegant, its arches cusped in the Mudéjar fashion. The vaulting of the apse of the basilica had turned early Gothic. In a casket on the altar lies St Isidore. Men and women were praying before the consecrated bread of the Holy Sacrament, exposed in a monstrance above the saint's baldacchino. For centuries the basilica of San Isidora has been granted the rare privilege of permanently exposing this Blessed Sacrament before the faithful.

It soon becomes apparent why Ferdinand I wished to bring the heavenly protection of St Isidore to this spot, for the basilica also shelters the tombs of himself and his royal line. Built between 1054 and 1066, this *Pantéon de los Reyes de Léon* displays such Mozarabic elements as palms and pineapples in its carved capitals. Here are the tombs of eleven kings, twelve queens and another twenty-one members of the Léon royal house. Isidore, alas, failed to protect their bones from the sacreligious behaviour of the French troops during the war of independence.

Around 1160 this pantheon was enormously enriched by some of the finest frescoes I have ever seen. The central vault is painted with a Byzantine-looking Christ Pantocrator, the elongated fingers of his right hand dramatically breaking into the mandorla surrounding him as he blesses us. A quaint feature of the four evangelists who surround him is the fact that Luke, John and Mark possess human bodies but their heads are transformed into the bull, the eagle and the lion that are their traditional symbols. Another entrancing section of these luminous paintings depicts the labours of each month. I speculated that either the labourers supposedly represent different men, or that an individual farmer depicted here was rich enough to bring out a new garment every month; but the obvious truth is that the unknown artists simply relished the different colours of their palettes, especially their blues, ochres and reds. In some scenes – angels proclaiming the good news of the Nativity to shepherds, for instance – animals abound, painted with an astonishing litheness. And where an unknown artist has depicted a couple of stags in ritual combat, the two of them forming a perfect pattern as they rise on their hind legs and their horns lock, somehow he has also managed to combine brilliant symmetry with a total realism.

Plateresque and Romanesque gave way to Gothic as I walked from San Isidoro to the cathedral of Santa María de la Regla. Although the citizens proudly dub their cathedral the beautiful Léonese (or *pulcra Leonina*), it is in fact the only Gothic building to have been influenced almost entirely by French models. Its west front is redolent of far-away Amiens (even to the extent of boasting different-sized towers) and its ground plan (with its three naves and triple transept) of distant Reims.

Before exploring the building it seemed to me time to take a large coffee and a snack in one of the bars nearby. To my surprise every space on its walls had been placarded with glossy, sometimes extremely moving Holy Week posters, collected in the previous year and drawn from many parts of the region. That of Léon itself showed black-robed men carrying a tableau of Jesus bearing his cross. The men of Zamora, bearing the body of the dead Jesus by candlelight, were distinguished by their bizarre masks and tall, pointed hats. A deathly statue of Jesus crucified and lying on a bed of roses announced the Holy Week processions of Salamanca.

Thus refreshed, spiritually as well as bodily, I went back to the cathedral. A late tenth-century palace once occupied the place on which it rises. Savagely ravaged by the forces of El Mansour, the palace was not rebuilt until the late eleventh century. It lasted a mere hundred years, demolished this time by the Christians, who wanted the site for their cathedral. Although Bishop Manrique de Lara laid the foundation stone in 1199, little was built for half a century. King Sancho IV who ruled from 1284 to 1295 enthusiastically supported the work, and Léon cathedral was consecrated in 1303.

In consequence the style is remarkably unified and uniformly graceful, with slender ogival vaulting. The centre of the nave rises to thirty-nine metres, almost exactly matching the width of the cathedral, while the building is ninety metres long. But the first delight that strikes anyone who walks inside is not this altogether magnificent interior but the thirteenth- and fourteenth-century stained glass, filling three major rose windows as well as another 1,500 or so square metres of the cathedral walls. The colours are varied and fresh, the lower glass depicting mostly sinuous plants, with angels and saints and knights in the lights higher up. The superb great rose window of the north transept (the fifteenth-century work of Jean d'Angers, whereas the rose of the west façade dates from the thirteenth) displays a delicacy of modulating colours as the rays of the lights spread out from the central depiction of the Madonna.

The cathedral furnishings are sumptuous. A massive screen depicts scenes from the nativity of Jesus. Evidence of the international nature of great art at this time are the mid-fifteenth-century choir stalls, seventy-six in all, sculpted in black walnut by Flemish woodcarvers. But the most luxurious spot in the whole cathedral is undoubtedly the chapel dedicated to St James. I discovered its sinuously carved entrance through a metal grille on the north side of the building. Juan de Badajoz built this chapel in the sixteenth century. Its stained glass is amongst the most luminous in the whole building. The roof is elegantly vaulted, and a frieze of stone acanthus leaves and mythical beasts, of angels and men, runs around the walls. On the pillars Samson wrestles with the lion, a stupid monk attempts to read and another giant writhes in the coils of a serpent. The so-called Virgin del Camiño stands on the altar, holding a huge, dead Jesus. St James himself sits in the centre of the richly sculpted Gothic niches on the wall behind.

I had not yet looked closely at the three splendid west entrances to Santa María de la Regla, which are so reminiscent of those at Reims and Amiens. The left portal is sculpted with scenes from the birth and infancy of Jesus: the visitation of Mary by the angel, the nativity itself, the adoration of the three Magi, the flight into Egypt and the massacre of the innocents. That on the right is devoted to the apotheosis of his mother: her coronation and dormition. The central doorway is dubbed the portal of Nuestra Señora la Blanca, a reference to the white stone of the Madonna who stands between the doors. Over her head in the tympanum is a Last Judgement. The saved listen to sacred music; the damned are horribly tortured, some eaten by demons, others boiling on cooking pots with a little figure vigorously working the bellows to keep the fires alive. The second statue to the right of Nuestra Señora la Blanca is St James, the only apostle wearing a hat, for he is on his pilgrim road. The column beneath him has been remarkably worn away, for over the centuries pilgrims have both repeatedly stroked it and rubbed it with their medallions, seeking a blessing before the final leg of their journey to Santiago de Compastela.

CHAPTER SIX

FROM LÉON TO THE CITY OF ST JAMES

LÉON – HOSPITAL DE ORBIGO – ASTORGA – PONFERRADA – CACABELOS – VILLAFRANCA DEL BIERZO – EL CEBRERO – TRIACASTELA – SAMOS – SARRIÁ – LUGO – PORTOMARIN – MELIDE – LAVACOLLA.

LEAVING LÉON, I drove across the medieval bridge by the Hospice of San Marcos and set out for Astorga by way of the countryside of Maragatos, a region named after an ancient tribe which inhabited it in pre-Roman times and whose descendants still live here. They were muleteers and traders, and their name – derived from an amalgam of Moorish and Visigothic words – means merchant. They needed to trade, for the land was not rich enough to support them simply from farming.

Five kilometres or so outside Léon a massive and graceless concrete cross incorporating a belfry fails to give the remotest impression of what the old pilgrimage crosses are like. As for the hideous new church, it was completed in 1961 to replace an eighteenth-century sanctuary dedicated to the *Virgen del Camiño*. Only the retable and the statue of the Virgin remain from the original building. On the façade hang modernistic statues of Mary and the twelve apostles. At least St James is recognizable by means of his pilgrim's staff. His right hand is said to point exactly towards Santiago de Compostela.

The first fifteen kilometres or so on the way to Astorga are as drab and harsh as this sanctuary. Beyond the sanctuary the chimneys of troglodyte homes pop up again, the first of what must be hundreds along the next few kilometres. At one point a recent re-routing of the N120 seems to have sliced through a whole village of them. These quaint homes, as well as the storks habitually perched on church towers, enlivened my route, which soon reached an infinitely more evocative spot than that of the Virgen del Camiño, namely Hospital de Orbigo. As its name suggests, pilgrims to Compostela could find shelter here, but only ruins remain of the former hospice. The medieval pilgrims' bridge here has been freed from road traffic by a new one built some hundred paces south, and its ochre stone arches, some pointed, some round, carry the ancient road a surprisingly long distance across to the other side of the Rio Orbigo. In 1434 this bridge was the venue for a celebrated joust, when one of the heroes of this region, Suero de Quiñones along with nine companions took on a similar number of opponents and – after a month of tournaments – defeated them according to the laws of chivalry. Having thus won over his lady, Doña Leonor Tovar, the victorious knight and his companions journeyed on to Compostela.

The countryside remains bleak, the least attractive of my whole journey to Compostela, though it is fertile enough to bear crops. And traditional methods of agriculture survive here to an astonishing degree. Halfway to Astorga I slowed down to negotiate the heavy modern bulldozers and huge trucks that were improving the road to Compostela. The contrast with what was going on in the fields to my left could not have been greater. A man was ploughing (or at least scraping the surface of the scrubland) by standing on a primitive plough and allowing himself to be pulled along by hanging on to his horse's tail. At the end of the field the nag stopped and turned around of its own accord. The ploughman spun his primitive plough, added his weight to it again and once more seized his horse's tail, at which the patient animal set off to the other side of the field. Meanwhile three other farmers were sowing the ploughed parts of the countryside. One carried a basket of seeds on his left arm, scattering them with his right (not an impossible task to perform evenly and methodically, as I know from my own farming childhood). A second walked beside him with a bag of seed, continually replenishing the basket, while a third man with a rake followed them, covering the seed with a layer of soil.

These scrublands eventually gave place to more fertile territory, with a few vineyards and orchards. I drove around a bend and suddenly saw ahead, rising on a hill across a valley of fruit trees and vines, the cathedral of Astorga, one tower pink the other grey, a foretaste of the curious mixture of materials to be seen in the whole building. As I later was to learn, apart from the west tower the pink bits are classical in design, the white mostly Gothic.

The road winds up into the centre of Astorga, and I parked in the shady square and was about to walk on to the cathedral when I met my first hikers on the road to Compostela. They were Germans, immaculately equipped with powerful boots, and they asked me in equally immaculate English when the banks opened. I was glad to help such intrepid pilgrims. Then, before I reached the cathedral, I visited the episcopal palace which Antonio Gaudí built beside it between 1887 and 1894. Its pure white granite walls add yet another hue to the stones of Astorga.

This palace is a far more resplendent example of Gaudí's genius than the Casa de los Botines at Léon. At Astorga the architect was at his most eclectic, mingling Gothic forms with art nouveau or *Modernista* sinuosity and with what he had adapted from his Mudéjar predecessors. Standing back from the palace you can see how Gaudí's insistence that all should fan out from a central space pulls the whole building together. The splayed arches of the porch by which I entered immediately set one's architectural spine tingling. Here the whole façade weaves an uncanny spell because its lines are never quite straight, its turrets are so spiky, its roofs seem so steep, its battlements incorporate such unexpected patterns and its shapes veer so unexpectedly.

What was more to the point of my pilgrimage, the palace today is a museum which houses a gallery devoted to the roads to Santiago de Compostela (the *museo de los Camiños*). A baroque statue of St James the apostle, book in hand, carrying his pilgrim's staff and wearing his upturned hat, welcomed me to this part of the palace. The exhibition includes maps of the many routes to Compostela. Drawn from churches and hospices throughout the region, other statues of St James depict him in a remarkable variety of poses, simple and complex, sometimes slaying Moors, sometimes piously reading, sometimes walking along as a pilgrim. Here are old photographs of genuine pilgrims as well as statues of idealized ones. A seventeenth-century Knight of St James rides to Compostela, dressed in the traditional pilgrim's garb. Gourds, staffs and drawings of the saint abound. My only complaints were that the place was freezingly cold and that very few of the exhibits were labelled. I bought a catalogue of the exhibition, but reading a catalogue while simultaneously visiting an exhibitions is as foolish as visiting Santa Croce in Florence with one's head lowered over a Baedeker.

The rest of the episcopal palace displays the genius of Antonio Gaudí at his most playful. The arches of the chapel are decorated in Mudéjar fashion with coloured ceramics. The bishop's throne room is suitably pompous. His dining room has stained glass windows in which is written a Latin grace. Staircases beckon with their sinuous twisting. And the whole exhibition is fascinating, with Santiago himself putting in more occasional appearances. In a room filled with medieval paintings one shows him alongside Jesus, who is reading the saint's epistle. St James wears a woolly hat into which a cockle-shell is fixed with hatpins. The cellars are filled with Roman sarcophagi, Roman coins and inscriptions, and the funeral effigy of a medieval knight lying on his tomb. Did the bishops of Astorga ever live here? If so, I hope they discovered the bathrooms and the bedrooms, for I did not. What I did find was a little alcove in which are drawings and photographs of the episcopal palace as Gaudí designed it and during its construction. Here too is a photograph of the genius in his prime, another showing him white-haired and fragile, and finally a drawing of the architect on his deathbed after he had been run over by a Barcelona tramcar in 1926.

Beside this palace powerful Gothic buttresses hold up Astorga's mostly fifteenth- and sixteenth-century cathedral. One tower remains unfinished, and both betray their eighteenth-century origin by their classical motifs. On the pinnacle of the apse stands a figure in baggy breeches who carries a flag. It represents Pero Mato, a legendary warrior who is said to have taken part in the battle of Clajivo and assisted Santiago in defeating the Moors. The rose-red west façade is tumultuously sculpted with religious motifs and anecdotes, the most animated scene being that in which Jesus drives money-changers out of the Jerusalem temple. Although the cathedral is dedicated to Our Lady, St James takes pride of place on the pediment over the main doorway, presiding over plateresque columns and pilasters.

The baroque of this façade gives way inside the cathedral to the Gothic of the soaring nave and aisles. Delicious lierne vaulting is enriched with gilded and painted bosses and pendentives. The cathedral is also blessed with magnificent Renaissance stalls, taking up the centre of the building and surrounding a massive bronze lectern. They were carved out of walnut in 1551 by two masters named Tomaso and Roberto. In the past, cathedral chapters often regarded much of the holy house as belonging exclusively to themselves and paid scant attention to the spiritual needs of anyone else who might wish to worship there. Nowhere is this seen better in Spain than in their habit of walling off most of the middle of a great church and cathedral and locking the laity out by means of ornamental metal screens. The stalls at Astorga cathedral were created precisely for this reason. Lazaro Azcain created the screens in 1622. Even today they are kept locked, but you can illuminate the two tiers of seats and their misericords by putting twenty-five pesetas into a slot near the screen – though in my case this device worked only when the verger came up and hit it.

A similar device illuminates the retable behind the high altar, a gilded sort of Grinling Gibbons affair. It was created in fact by the most gifted of all sixteenth-century Spanish woodcarvers, Gaspar Beccara, who had worked in Rome, learning from such masters as Daniel de Volterra and Michelangelo. This retable is his masterpiece, created for Astorga cathedral between 1158 and 1569.

The modern organ of the cathedral has a case which is pleasingly in keeping with the rest of the building. At the west end is an astronomical clock, which you pass on the way to the cloisters. These were rebuilt in the classical style in 1780 by Gaspar Lopez. The garden which they enclose has a deep well, for Astorga rises high above the surrounding plain.

Once Astorga boasted twenty-five pilgrims' hospices and inns. The sole remaining one stands in the cathedral square. Dedicated to San Juan, it was founded in the twelfth century, though the present little building dates from the eighteenth. I walked from it to the plaza Mayor, a square of porticoes and balconies which is shaded by a lovely Renaissance town hall. Its baroque belfry flanked by a couple of Renaissance towers is more ornate. The two mechanical figures who ring the hours are dressed in the traditional costumes of the Maragatos. Then I walked around the ramparts of the city. Astorga, which stands where four Roman roads meet, was founded by the Romans and known to them as Asturica Augusta. Pliny went so far as to describe the town as 'urbs magnifica', and these ramparts were built by his compatriots.

As I drove around these Roman ramparts I paused for a while and realized how sympathetically the apse of Gaudí's episcopal palace (which is designed as a Greek cross) respects the Gothic apse of the cathedral. I wondered where he obtained his pure white granite, a question almost immediately answered, for I found myself driving through granite country. The scenery was steadily improving. The hills, heather and dry-stone walls reminded me of Dartmoor, though Dartmoor as yet is not dotted with vineyards or too many fir plantations. Occasionally a slag heap appeared, for this is coal-mining country. Ahead appeared a snow-capped Sierra. I followed the new road, which tunnels through the mountains. The only fault of this road is that at the 1225-metres Monzanal pass it no longer runs beside the ancient pilgrims' hospice.

The road descends, and shortly I made a little detour south to see Bembibre, not for its ruined castle but because the Romanesque church here is said to be a converted synagogue. If it is, one would never guess simply from looking at it. Just outside the town is a monastery, San Miguel de las Dueñas, which was founded in the tenth century.

Approaching Ponferrada through an ugly industrialized suburb, I spotted the signpost directing travellers to the right to reach the tenth-century Mozarabic church of San Tomás de la Ollas. Immediately I was plunged from the industrial life of the twentieth-century into a tiny hamlet that seems not to have changed for centuries. The houses have tumbling wooden balconies, some of them overhanging dangerously, I thought. As for the ancient church, it is built out of different-coloured granite and has a narrow belfry that could hang three bells but houses only two. Neither seems to be rung today, for a loudspeaker on the roof broadcasts recorded bells to summon the villagers to divine worship. The church was locked, but I knocked on a door and was told that a lady named Amelia kept the key. She lived at number 7, a house with a green-painted balcony close by the church. Amelia, in apron, green-shaded spectacles and slippers, willingly left her lunch to show me inside the church. Its Romanesque doorway opens on to steps leading to the former ground level. The church, said Amelia, is domed like a mosque. The right-hand chapel is supported on keyhole-shaped arches, the east end, with its little classical reredos, is decidedly Mozarabic, and the font – like the rest of the church – is made of granite. So I gave Amelia a tip and she told me to have a good day.

Situated at the confluence of the Rivers Boeza and Sil, Ponferrada itself is a much grander spot, and happily has not been invaded by the industrialization of its suburbs. You reach it by crossing a medieval bridge over the Boeza. The Romans called Ponferrada 'Interamnium Flavium', and it derives its present name (which means 'iron bridge') from its position on the road to Santiago. The Romans had built a bridge across the River Sil, and in the eleventh century Bishop Osmundo of Astorga strengthened it with iron railings to help the pilgrims across. I found the tenth-century church of Santiago, which much resembles that at Santo Tomás de la Ollas, but this time I could find no one to unlock the door. So I parked in the arcaded plaza de Ayuntamiento in front of the baroque town hall, which was built in 1652 as the palace of Reynardo Carlos II. From here the arch of a clock-tower, which was once Ponferrada's medieval watchtower and is all that remains of the city's fortifications, opens into a narrow, shady street with some very grand doorways, one of them belonging to a convent of the Immaculate Conception which was built in 1542. The street leads into a square across which rises the basilica of Santa María de la Encina, but that too was locked, so I walked on to the fortress which the Templars built in the twelfth and thirteenth centuries to protect the pilgrims.

King Ferdinand II of Léon gave the Templars the town in 1185. They were expelled from it in 1312, their last bastion in Spain. Although ruined, their castle is a most impressive fortress, with evocative battlemented walls, round and square bastions and a moat. A flag was flying over the superb entrance to the fortress, which is reached by three stepped and battlemented walls and turns out to be not just one gateway but three, the second with a portcullis. Inside is everything you could desire in a ruined castle: living quarters, fragments of a chapel, a ruined keep, a well. There are well-worn paths through the grass, but for some reason that day I was there alone save for the pigeons.

On a nearby building a couple of coats of arms, one with cockleshells, indicate that this was once the Hospice de la Reina, a hospice paid for by Queen Isabella the Catholic in 1498 to shelter pilgrims on their way through the valley of the Bierzo. As I walked back to my car I realized I was following the parish priest, who must just have finished lunch, and he unlocked the basilica of Nuestra Señora de la Encina. Founded by the Templars in the twelfth century on the spot where the Blessed Virgin Mary had appeared in an oak tree, it was partly rebuilt in 1577, and also has a fine classical entrance and carries an elaborate baroque belfry. Inside are no fewer than five reredoses: a classical one behind the high altar, flanked by a couple more with twisting baroque columns; a simpler one on the south wall; and on the north wall another sculpted with a stupendous baroque version of the resurrection, the damned being whipped into flames while above them the saved rise sweetly into the arms of God.

The route to Compostela continues from Ponferrada through extensive vineyards to reach Cacabelos, which is a beguiling spot. Here I paused by an arcaded little square with tiny old houses and a modern statue of a happy wine-growing family, parents and two children walking back from their vineyard, the father carrying grapes in a wicker basket, his daughter eating a bunch of grapes. The plaza Mayor is green-grassed and tree-shaded. The church of Santa María was unlocked for a funeral. The mourners emerged watched from the top of the tower by an indifferent stork. Though it does make a pretence at the Romanesque, this tower fits ill on the twelfth- to sixteenth-century church, and an obtrusive plaque affixed to it declares that it was paid for in 1904 by Don José and Don Jorge Roderiguez. The pillars inside the church are powerful and rectangular.

Two ladies who had been attending the funeral pointed me the way to the eighteenth-century hospice and sanctuary of La Quinta Augusta. The walk took me down a charming narrow street north of the church, a street called the way of Sorrows (calle de las Angustias), which is a reference to the seven sorrows of Mary. It leads to a three-arched bridge over the Rio Cúa, on which a scarcely decipherable inscription proclaims that it was built by the Emperor Charles v. Across the bridge is a mill driven by the stream, a dovecote built into its upper storey. Beyond it rises the imposing façade of the hospice, on top of which two storks were nesting. Over its porch is a crowned Virgin Mary with her dead son in her lap, a statue representing her fifth sorrow I suppose (though my own breviary numbers this as her sixth). At the opposite side of the road stands one of the most ramshackle houses I have ever seen, still inhabited, with a wooden balcony, a vine trailing around the walls and an ancient slate roof covered in moss. The hospice was locked, so I walked behind it to sit for a while on a bench under the trees of a little park.

Then I drove on through lovely hilly country, studded with fruit trees and vineyards, and after eight kilometres saw ahead the late fifteenth-century fortress which defends Villafranca del Bierzo, massive round towers at each of its corners. The town nestles in the foothills of the Sierra de Ancares. Parking opposite the door of the fortress, whose conical roofs and battlements are made less stern by the Renaissance elements which were creeping into architecture when it was built, I walked up to the stern church of Santiago, which was guarded by a sleepy sheepdog. This proved to be the one place where I decided that the demands of tourism have taken the cult of Santiago over the top. The custodian appeared with a cockle-shell hanging from his key. The interior of the church is lit with bulbs set in wrought-iron cockle-shell holders. Less off-putting, though modern, is the statue of St James, dressed as a pilgrim. The church remains completely romanesque, with a single nave and a wide, columned choir. The twelfth-century north porch is splendidly decorated, and used to be known as the portal of mercy (or *peurta del pardón*), a reference to the tradition that sick pilgrims who flagged here on the way to Compostela could be absolved at Santiago de Villafranca del Bierzo without journeying any further.

From outside the rusty-coloured walls of this church you can see over to the Romanesque church of San Francesco, with its two classical towers. Walking down into the town, I climbed up again to the church, but this one was firmly locked. Villafranca del Bierzo is a picturesque town, which prospered on the pilgrim route, so that not only the Francescans but also the Jesuits came here. Their baroque church rises in the main square, a statue of St Ignatius Loyola over its thirteenth-century Romanesque porch and the monastic buildings next door still intact. The façade is enlivened with broken pediments and sculpted pomegranates (a sure sign of Moorish architects). This church stands on the site of the former Hospice of St Roch and is the pantheon of the Counts of Villafranca, who built the town's fortress.

Beyond the square is a formal garden, and west of it beside the river is the collegiate church of Santa María de Cluniaco. In 1220 the monks who ran it were granted a tenth of the tolls charged on pilgrims who passed through the town. In the early sixteenth century the Counts of Villafranca del Bierzo rebuilt it. Roderigo Gil de Hontañon, who was then working on Astorga cathedral, had a hand in its design. Today's church is constructed out of granite whose colour subtly changes, with massive chased limestone pillars holding up delicate stone arches. Its dome has a little walkway with what seems an extraordinarily fragile railing. It was two o'clock in the afternoon when I arrived, and a confraternity consisting entirely of men was singing an office in the chancel. So I sat in the sculpted classical stalls and listened to them. Over every seat of these stalls is a cherub, and on the coat of arms at the west end of the stalls are cockle-shells. When the office was over, one of the men came to pick up his hat, which he had left on the stalls. He told me that this was the most splendid church in Villafranca del Bierzo and showed me how you can see from the unfinished western pillars that it was planned to be even larger. I forgot to ask him what was the confraternity he belonged to.

The name Villafranca indicates that this town (and its Cluniac monks) especially welcomed French pilgrims. Their route took them down one of its most charming streets, the calle d'Agua, which is narrow and boasts some noble houses with overhanging balconies and the coats of arms of the grandees who once lived in them sculpted on the walls. I left the town by taking the medieval bridge over the River Burbia and experienced an exhilarating mountain drive into Galicia and as far as Piedrafita do Cebrero, where I turned left to climb to the sanctuary of El Cebrero. As I started to climb there appeared spectacular panoramas of the surrounding countryside, until it suddenly started to rain, and then to snow. A pilgrimage cross appeared through the blizzard and then a sign pointing to the summit of the peak and the *Santuario del Cebrero*. Parking in the square formed by the sanctuary buildings, I fled from the snow into the hospice, conscious for the first time of the reason why the pilgrims needed thick cloaks and wide-brimmed hats.

This is one of the most fascinating places on the whole pilgrimage route. The dry-stone buildings at the summit of the pass of O Cebrero, which is almost 1,300 metres above sea-level, are prehistoric – circular in shape with conical roofs which till recently were made of thatch. Even their church is pre-Romanesque. If any place required a pilgrims' hostel this one did, and one was founded here as early as 836. In 1072, under the patronage of King Alfonso VI, it was affiliated to the celebrated Benedictine abbey which St Géraud had founded in the tenth century at Aurillac in the Auvergne, and the chapel is still dedicated to San Geraldo. French monks continued to serve the hospice till 1487, when the Spanish monarchy, in its determination to stamp out any foreign influence in its realms, expelled them and placed El Cebrero under the guardianship of the monastery of San Benito de Valladolid.

The monks of San Benito abandoned El Cebrero in 1853, and by the 1960s most of the village and hospice was in ruins. Today it has been perfectly restored. The hospice has become a modern hostel. The restaurant in which I found myself, with its long communal tables and many pictures of St James on its walls, seemed exactly what a pilgrim should expect. One of the women who runs it let me into the church, which is connected to the hostel by a covered way. Although over the centuries the monks modified the church at El Cebrero, they never rebuilt it or destroyed its basic character. Its porch is mighty. Beside the altar is a primitive form of sedilia, where the priests and their assistants would sit during Mass. The font, designed for baptism by total immersion, dates from the thirteenth century.

In the late thirteenth century or very early in the fourteenth this chapel and El Cebrero became famous because of a miracle which has passed into European legend. Each day a shepherd from the nearby hamlet of Barxamajor would walk to the hospice church for Mass. One morning the blizzard was so fierce that the indolent priest hoped the man would not appear. When the faithful shepherd arrived, the priest remarked that he must be a fool to walk in such weather to worship simple bread and wine. As he said this, the bread of the Holy Eucharist was transformed into flesh and the wine in the chalice turned into blood. Pilgrims carried the tale back with them, and it became incorporated into the legend of the Holy Grail, the mysterious vessel said to have been used by Jesus at the last supper and still containing drops of his blood, a legend which Chrétien de Troyes had recently immortalized in his *Conte del Graal*. The full name of the sanctuary thus became El Cebrero do Danto Grail. The same twelfth-century chalice and paten used by the priest when the miracle occured is still on display in the chapel of the miracle of the Eucharist, the paten slightly battered, the chalice a beautiful example of Romanesque craftsmanship. The custodians of this spot have bathed it in an eerie ultramarine glow. This chapel itself seems to me a miracle of Romanesque construction, with massive stones in its arches and a wall built of multi-shaped pieces fixed together like an architectural jigsaw.

As for the transformed bread and wine, these too are preserved at El Cebrero. Queen Isabella of Spain wished to take them elsewhere, it is said, but the mules charged with their transport refused to budge.

The crystal reliquary in which they are displayed today was a gift of the Catholic kings of Spain in 1486. As for the twelfth-century statue of the Virgin Mary in this chapel, the lady who had let me in says that she inclines her head in acknowledgement of the wondrous miracle. Rather than bending her head, to me she seemed to be concentrating on balancing on it the absurd crown that someone has thought fit to put on this elegant Madonna, as well as holding in her lap her over-sized, curly-haired baby.

The next village on is called Hospital, which must surely denote that there was once a hospice here. I drove over the 1327-metre peak of Santa María del Poyo and emerged from the blizzard to see panoramas of mountain crests and a countryside strewn with gorse and silver birches. At Triacastela the route meets the River Sarriá. The church here has a Romanesque apse and a tall, classical tower, and Triacastela also boasts a pilgrims' hospice that incoporates a pilgrims' gaol. French prisoners long ago carved cocks on its walls. Just outside Triacastela is a pilgrimage cross with a pile of stones at its base, a remembrance of the time when pilgrims were asked to carry a limestone rock from here to Compostela, where it would be turned into lime for rebuilding the cathedral.

In the valley of the poplar-lined river limestone rocks have weathered into fantastic shapes. The next village, Samos, held a delightful surprise, for it is almost entirely dominated by an enormous Benedictine monastery. Its baroque façade is like the entrance to a grandiose château, approached by a monumental staircase and betraying its monastic nature only by a couple of bells hanging in the upper storey and a statue of St Benedict over the doorway.

On a side door a notice gave the times when a tour of the monastery is allowed. I had arrived ten minutes before opening time, so I walked on into the village to buy myself a bottle (or, as it turned out, a carton) of white *vino de meso* for the evening. On the way I passed the tenth-century village church, partly Mozarabic Romanesque in style, as well as a pilgrimage cross.

Returning to the monastery, I was welcomed by a bald, charming monk in his brown tunic. He was exactly what you want a monk to be, adoring his monastery and exuding warmth. When I told him about the blizzard at El Cebrero, he laughed and laughed. His monastery, though huge, has an air of intimacy, for it is cunningly divided into many quiet spaces and quarters. In the middle of the greater cloister is a formal garden of palm trees and roses, with a statue of Brother P. Feijóo, who, my guide said, was a famous eighteenth-century writer and member of his order. This cloister is built in the Renaissance style, whereas the late Gothic smaller cloister has a Romanesque doorway – one of the few parts of the monastery dating from its foundation, by monks from Toledo and Córdoba, in the thirteenth century. (Some say, I should add here, that this monastery based itself on a sixth-century one, but many historians consider this unlikely.) In this cloister I was happy to discover cockle-shells on some of the bosses of the vaulting, but my guide pointed to his own favourite device: a boss in the shape of an insect. The garden of the smaller cloister boasts a splendid baroque fountain in the shape of sea-nymphs, who sport massive breasts.

We climbed to the upper storey of the great cloister, around which three modern artists have painted a huge fresco of the life of St Benedict. In 1960 José Luis was commissioned to paint scenes from the saint's early life. These include Totila the Goth submitting to Benedict, who had rebuked him for planning to ravage Italy, and another of Benedict overthrowing a pagan temple at Montecassino. As he pointed to a fresco of an impudent-looking demon, the eyes of my guide twinkled impishly. The artist Celia Cortés continued the painting in 1961, and the fresco was finished by Enrice Navarro in 1964. Here are silhouettes of Montecassino, where the monastery which Benedict founded became one of the most famous in Christendom. Benedict is seen performing all manner of wonders, for example curing an epileptic. Celia Cortés even includes a pastiche of a painting by Goya idealizing the saint. Benedict appears writing his *Regula monasteriorum*, the rule which to this day remains the basis of every monastic discipline. One long fresco depicts the saint expounding his rule to modern friends of Samos monastery. The bishops, Pope, monks and laity are, said my guide, idealized portraits, though the hook-nosed abbot painted here is a genuine portrait of his late superior. The cycle ends with an angel taking the soul of Benedict into heaven.

We went into the vestibule of the monastery church, a modern Gothic building frescoed with scenes from the life of Jesus, and on into the octagonal baroque sacristy, vestment chests under its dome. There were many of these chests, and I asked my guide how many monks lived here nowadays. His face became sad as he said, 'Only eleven.' 'The sea of faith ebbs and flows,' I said. Then we went into the three-naved classical church. Its retable with Corinthian columns and the clouds of heaven has lost its altar, the result of the liturgical reforms which oblige priests to celebrate Mass facing the people rather than facing east. The date of this church can be readily spotted, for over the retable left on the south side is written 1734, when building began, and over that on the north side is written 1748, when it ended. The architect of this rather glamorous building was a monk of

Samos, Brother Juan Velázquez. One of the four learned theologians who appear just beneath the cupola is St Anselm, who was Archbishop of Canterbury from 1093 to 1109. He is depicted here wearing golden spectacles.

Many pilgrims to Compostela died hereabouts, said the monk, and are buried in the graveyard of his monastery. As I left he took me warmly by the hand and refused any payment for my guided tour. Twelve kilometres further on I reached Sarriá. I discovered its ruined medieval fortress by following the signs to the Mosteiro de la Magdalena. The convent itself, founded in the thirteenth century, was once a pilgrims' hospice. It has preserved a Romanesque-Gothic cloister and its church boasts a Renaissance façade. Sarriá is also blessed with the Romanesque church of El Salvador, whose tympanum is sculpted with the figure of Jesus. A bull of Pope John XXII, still extant and preserved in the national archive at Madrid, was sent to this church in 1332, offering indulgences to anyone who aided a pilgrim to Compostela. It was little help to King Alfonso IX of Castile, who was intent on passing through here on his way to Compostela but instead dropped dead.

Beside the roads in this part of Galacia are signposts marking the Camiño de Santiago, and that at Sarriá points you in the direction of Portomarin. However, I had no intention of passing up a visit to the finest surviving city walls in Spain, so I drove instead north-west to Lugo. Lugo, which was probably founded by the Celts (since Lug was their fire god) is an exceedingly prosperous city, well laid out, with paved streets and grand houses as well as a medieval quarter. Raimundo de Montforte began building its present cathedral in 1120 on the site of an eighth-century church, modelling the new one on the cathedral of Santiago. On the north side a Gothic portico shelters a Romanesque archway above which sits a crowned and enthroned Jesus. The twin spires are classical in style, and the façade was given a classical-Renaissance look in 1769. The interior is a similar mixture of styles, the result of continual rebuilding, so that a classical apse jostles a Romanesque aisle, a baroque reredos and sixty-six baroque stalls sculpted by Francesco Moure in the 1630s. Even more ornamental is the sacristy, the creation of Domingo de Andrade in 1670, and the altarpiece of Miguel de Romay containing the statue of Our Lady of the Large Eyes, patroness of the city. I arrived at Lugo cathedral at eight o'clock on a wet Thursday evening to find the place filled with worshippers.

Behind the cathedral stands the episcopal palace, with its fine balcony, built for Bishop Gil Taboada in 1738. From the arcaded and triangular plaza del Campo, with its mid-eighteenth century fountain whose statue represents St Vincent Ferrar (who was born in the mid-fourteenth century of an English father and a Spanish mother), I followed rúa Nova to reach plaza del Soledad and the church of San Francesco. Traditionally St Francis of Assisi himself is said to have founded this monastic church when he was returning to Italy after a pilgrimage to Compostela. Much of the monastery has gone, but beside the Gothic church with its lovely rose window the cloisters still preserve Romanesque capitals on their pillars, while other monastic buildings now house the provincial museum.

Before exploring the walls I rested in the medieval quarter of the city (the *rinconade del Miño*) in a bar whose waitress spoke excellent English and resembled the Hollywood actor Jack Palance, who usually played the villain in westerns. A song by Sammy Davis Junior came over the loudspeaker and she told me she had seen him perform at a place called Caesar's Palace. 'At Las Vegas?' I enquired. 'No, in Luton,' came her surprising reply. Refreshed, I went to look at the walls of Lugo, undoubtedly the most splendid example of defensive architecture in Spain. All 2,130 metres of them were built by the Romans in the third century AD. They were once buttressed by no fewer than eight-five towers, some of them with gates, many still remaining intact. The oldest are the Miña, Falsa and Nova towers, and the tower of Santiago. Over the Santiago gateway rides an eighteenth-century image of Santiago Matamaros.

From Lugo the road winds south through twenty-six kilometres of well-cultivated fields to Portomarín. The countryside is wooded, and slate fences divide up the fields like little tombstones laid end to end. There in the hotel known as the Mesón de Rodríguez I met a truly determined group of hikers. German Catholics from Oberhausen near Düsseldorf, they had driven in a minibus as far as Ponferrada. Each evening they sat down to work out their next station, some twenty kilometres or so away. The next day half of the party would drive off in the minibus to find lodgings, while the rest walked the pilgrimage route, all meeting later at a pre-arranged spot.

This was a homely hotel. The menu had been painted and then fired on a plate, a sign that no one planned to change it for several years. A fat and happy black-haired baby lay in a cot by the bar, happy for he was continually smothered in love and kisses from his mother and grandmother. The mother even carried the infant on her arm as she served my pudding in the restaurant. At one point she also brought me a litre of *Ribeiro denominación de origen blanco* which was really destined for the Germans, and then whisked it away amid much merriment, for I was already sipping half a bottle of my own.

In the morning the Germans put on their superb hiking boots,

shook hands (politely taking off their hats as they did so) and set off
for their next stage while I investigated Portomarín. This is a town
saved from drowning. Around 1120 the wide River Miño above
which it stands was spanned by a bridge some 150 metres long. Later
in the century the Knights of St John took over the town and built a
fortress-church for themselves, dedicated to San Juan. Around it the
village grew and prospered. In 1962 it was decided to dam the river in
order to create the Belesar reservoir. The project completely flooded
the old town, but before this happened its chief monuments were
moved stone by stone up the hill to a new site. What was one of
Spain's charmingly decrepit towns became the present gleaming spot,
its cobbled streets and squares a re-creation of a medievel town. Some
medieval houses and palaces, in particular the arcaded seventeenth-
century Palacio de Berbetoros which stands in the main square, were
saved from the waters; but the most remarkable monument rebuilt in
the centre of modern Portomarin is the fortified church of San Juan.
This is a square building, its roof battlemented, with slits in its walls
for shooting at enemies. On the main doorway above which is a rose
window, the twenty-four elders of the Apocalypse are carved, each
playing his instrument in the heavenly choir in honour of Christ Pantocrator who also sits here. The south porch is equally ravishing,
depicting St Nicholas with two assistants who carry his book and his
staff. Further down the hill is the church of San Pedro, its late
twelfth-century medieval porch also saved from the waters.

Portomarín was given a new bridge when the river was dammed,
and from it I looked down at the skeleton of the old town, its crumbling houses revealed by the low waters, along with the stump of an
arch which once carried the pilgrims' bridge of 1120. On the corner
by the bridge is a pilgrimage cross, Christ crucified carved on one
side, the Madonna and Child on the other.

I left the town by way of the C535, turned towards Lugo and
shortly turned left along the C547 and the Camiño de Santiago. At
Vilar de Doñas I turned right along a narrow road to find after two
and a half kilometres another treat on this pilgrimage, the Romanesque church of a monastery which once welcomed travellers to this
spot. Outside it is a pilgrimage cross.

Only three pointed arches remain from its former cloister. The
splendid Romanesque porch of the church is decorated with flowers
and a zigzag dog-tooth pattern, with grapes and sheaves of corn.
Above it are three figures. In the centre St Michael holds the scales
with which he judges the sins and virtues of the dead. On the left is
the Madonna, and on the right St Bartholomew (or is it John the Baptist?). The ancient door preserves its medieval metalwork.

Inside the church I regretted the smell of mould and mildew, for this is one of the most precious relics of the pilgrimage road to Compostela. The monastery at Vilar de Doñas was founded by two saintly and noble ladies (the *Doñas*) around the middle of the twelfth century and given by them to the Knights of St James. These continued to extend the church until the mid-thirteenth century. It became the pantheon of those Galician members of the Order killed in combat with the Moors. Some of their medieval tomb slabs are still here, as well as a couple of effigies of fallen knights. One knight's tomb is held up by two friendly-looking lions.

The pavement of the church actually descends as you walk towards the Romanesque crossing and triple apse, where there are some Gothic tombs and a Gothic baldacchino in the north transept. This church has a clover-leaf apse, and in the middle behind the altar is a striking fresco, painted in 1434. It depicts the two donors of the church and a moving Resurrection. Jesus is emerging from a coffin, still bleeding, both from the wounds of his crucifixion and from those he suffered when he was flogged. The spear which pierced his side is three times depicted, and the artist has painted two lashes, hanging on either side of the suffering Redeemer. On the granite altar a Romanesque carving depicts the Deposition, the Resurrection, and most fascinating of all, a scene of a priest celebrating the Eucharist which is almost certainly a reference to the miracle of El Cebrero. The priest gazes at his risen Lord, while an altar boy (or perhaps the troublesome shepherd) holds a book.

Just as I was about to leave I spotted a Romanesque stoop and also, under the round bowl of the Romanesque font, four cockleshells. Then I returned to the C547 and drove on to Palas de Rei. The Gothic King Witiza built a palace here in the first decade of the eighth century, and popular tradition has it that the place derives its name from this. In truth the title goes back only as far as King Alfonso xi of Galicia and Léon, who granted the town the use of his title. The parish church of San Tirso here has preserved its Romanesque porch, and the statue on the town fountain is St James. Cockle-shells adorn some of its medieval houses, as well as its neat modern milestone.

I now wanted to find the celebrated medieval castle of Pambre, and beyond Palas de Rei, just after the village of Orosa, spotted a signpost saying that a *castello* stood six kilometres away to the left, along the road to Pedraza. The route twists and turns, plunging into and emerging from richly varied forest, passing forgotten hamlets (one of them with a pilgrimage cross), crossing little streams. The sign for Pambre took me to the right, driving up what ceased to be a metalled road and became little better than a farm-track. The sight of the incredibly decrepit fourteenth-century fortress was worth all the trouble of finding it. Vegetation was growing from its machicolated keep and turrets, and creepers climbed up its white stone walls. I walked down to it, and was delighted to find that the gate opened easily. Inside, I was amazed to discover that the place is inhabited. No one was there at the time, only a bicycle, a cement mixer and the debris of everyday life in the courtyard. In the middle of this courtyard was one of the remarkable granaries of this part of Spain, a long stone oblong, raised from the ground on stone stilts, with slits wide enough to let in the air and keep the grain fresh but narrow enough to keep out unwelcome birds who might want a free feed.

The dirt track I had followed continued halfway up a bare hillside with a steep drop to the right. As I drove gingerly on, it suddenly became a properly surfaced road again. Delving into the valley, it passed another pilgrimage cross as a sharp right-turn took me winding back to the main road. I left it again to visit the hamlets of Leboreiro and Furelos, for this was the route medieval pilgrims took. The name of the first hamlet derives from the Latin 'Campus Levurarius', which means camp of hares. In the centre of the village is an ancient pilgrimage cross on a sculpted plinth, and the stone-walled houses all seem to have been restored. In front of the pretty Romanesque church of Santa María stands a former hospice, a coat of arms on its façade. I liked the Gothic tympanum of the church. The pointed arch which shields it still has a Romanesque dog-tooth pattern. In the tympanum the infant Jesus stands on the lap of a hieratic Madonna, worshipped by people half her size. A pilgrims' bridge with a single arch spans the tiny, tree-shaded River Seco.

Between here and Furelos I was treated to the sight of an old lady leading two oxen which pulled a cart in which her husband stood, beret on head and leaning on his stick. Was he perhaps a cripple, or did he traditionally expect the womenfolk to do most of the work? At Furelos the Seco is crossed by a beautiful five-arched Gothic bridge, the irregular brown stones of its walls contrasting with the smooth white stones of its round arches.

My next pause was at the Romanesque church of San Pedro, at the entrance to Melide. Its porch is satisfying and simple. On the classical retable is a statue of St Roch, as usual showing his suppurating leg and accompanied by the dog that saved his life. The dog carries a stolen bun in its mouth. Roch is fascinatingly dressed as a Santiago pilgrim, a cockle-shell in his wide-brimmed hat, two more on his cloak. He carries his pilgrim's staff and his water bottle, and he is wearing sturdy hiking-boots. When the church authorities decreed that priests must celebrate Holy Communion facing the people, at Samos, as I noted with some sadness, the high altar was taken away. Here someone has come up with a better solution, transforming the Romanesque font into a free-standing altar. San Pedro also houses the tomb of a medieval knight.

Outside the church is a beautiful fourteenth-century pilgrimage cross, the oldest in Galicia. One side depicts Jesus crucified, flanked by his mother and St John. His legs are crossed, pinned to the cross by a single nail driven through both of them. On the other side, though his hands are still nailed to the cross, Christ reigns from the tree in glory. This remarkable cross stands in a very pretty garden, with tree-ferns, palms, rose trees and flowers.

Opposite the town hall of Melide is the seventeenth-century porch of the parish church, all that remains of the Hospice of the Holy Spirit, set up in 1375 with, as records tell us, twelve beds in which slept twenty-four pilgrims. This church boasts a gilded reredos with twisting baroque columns, which unfortunately conceals some sixteenth-century frescoes. At the other end of the town, virtually hidden on the left, stands Melide's third church, the twelfth-century Santa María. Once it was the chapel of the convent which ran the pilgrims' hospice of the Holy Spirit. In the churchyard stands another pilgrimage cross, much simpler than that outside San Pedro, just as the porch of Santa María is also much simpler than San Pedro's. An alcove in the wall was obviously designed to house a scene from the events of Holy Week, but the niche is empty.

The building was locked, but a crippled lady emerged from the house next to it and kindly hobbled to the other end of the street to fetch the custodian, who unlocked it for me. One of the capitals in the apse depicts Daniel in the lion's den, while the other is sculpted with leaves. The Romanesque altar is decorated with little arches and seems to have retained some of its original paint. And behind it is a medieval wall painting of the Holy Trinity – God the Father, Christ crucified, and the Holy Spirit in the form of a dove – surrounded by the four evangelists and six apostles. I envied St John's full head of red hair and resigned myself to looking more like the grey-haired, tonsured St Peter. Beside them angels are playing long trumpets, horns and medieval trombones.

Melide is where the citizens of Santiago de Compostela came to welcome a new archbishop on his way there from Rome, and I, like such an archbishop, was very close to my goal; but I had decided to make one more diversion. Taking the C549 north-west towards Betanzos, I turned right at Corredoiras to find the stately grey walls and baroque towers of the Cistercian monastery of Sobrado dos Monxes. Founded in 1142 and extensively rebuilt in the sixteenth and eighteenth centuries, its magnificent church has a baroque façade designed in the late seventeenth century by Pedro de Monteagudo.

The stupendously arched interior is chiefly the work of Domingo de Andrade, who became architect after the death of Pedro in the early eighteenth century. Domingo de Andrade did not destroy everything from the earlier church. The choir was sculpted by Gregorio Español and Juan Davila in the late sixteenth century. The sacristy, the chapel of the rosary and the chapel of San Juan were built to the designs of Domingo de Monteagudo in the 1670s.

This monastery still retains three eighteenth-century cloisters, as well as the medieval kitchen and chapterhouse; and Sobrado also boasts a parish church with a sixteenth-century crucifix by a pupil of Juan de Juni. Another lovely monastic church stands some twenty kilometres further north-west along the C540 at Mezonzo, which lies just to the left of the road. The Romanesque church of Santa María de Mezonzo is all that remains of a monastery founded here in 986 by St Pedro de Mezonzo, Archbishop of Compostela, to whom is attributed the hymn to the Blessed Virgin, *Salve Regina*.

I drove back to Corredoiras and turned south-west to reach Arzúa on the C547 again. At Arzúa the Romanesque church is dedicated to Santiago, and close by the Gothic chapel of La Magdalena stands what once was a pilgrims' hospice, founded by the Augustinians of Sarriá in the fourteenth century.

Medieval pilgrims made one last stop before reaching Santiago de Compostela. The spot, Lavacolla, which has given its name to Santiago's airport, boasts a baroque church and simple calvary. Aimery Picaud called it Lavamentula. Here, he tells us, 'pilgrims washed not only their faces, but also, out of love for St James, took off their clothing and washed their whole bodies, cleaning away every spot of dirt.' Then the pilgrims would race to the top of Monte del Gozo, the mount of joy, to gain their first view of Santiago. The first member of any party to reach the spot would often claim the privilege of adding to his name the surname 'king', hence the names Leroi, Leroy, Rey and Roy.

A seventeenth-century Italian priest named Domenico Laffi, who made no fewer than three separate pilgrimages to Santiago, has left an account of himself and his fellow-pilgrims falling to their knees here and singing the *Te Deum* with tears of joy running down their faces. Those who were on horseback, he tells us, made the rest of the journey on foot, and others took of their shoes for the final leg. I drove on, and my first view of Santiago de Compostela was simply three towers rising over such urban sprawl and high-rise horror that I momentarily felt like turning back.

CHAPTER SEVEN

SANTIAGO DE COMPOSTELA

Santiago de compostela, in spite of its unseemly suburbs, has survived into the twentieth century as an amazingly beautiful city, with little winding streets as well as wide and noble ones, with great squares and hidden corners, and with a fine and sometimes superb building at almost every turn. I drove through the suburbs, and they quite suddenly disappeared, as the little hermitage of San Gaetano appeared on the left. Almost immediately afterwards I reached the heart of the ancient city.

As that distinguished American scholar of the Romanesque, A. Kingsley Porter, wrote in the 1920s, such is the singular poetry of the place that 'one feels, as nowhere else, wrapped about by the beauty of the Middle Age.' He found what he described as 'an inner vitality, whether poetic or spiritual I know not, but still forcibly living at Santiago, and unquenchably beautiful there; beautiful none the less because seen across swarms of well-fed priests and a pestilence of syphilitic beggars, just as the living Romanesque core of the basilica shines out through an external coating of barocco, fine, too, in its way, yet writhing in an agony of dissolution.' Apart from approving of priests being fed properly and not knowing anything about the medical condition of the beggars of Santiago, I entirely agree.

Compostela still keeps alive the myth that St Francis of Assisi made a pilgrimage to visit the bones of its patron saint, and you enter the city centre by way of a Franciscan church and convent and past an excellent modern memorial to ths saint of Assisi, sculpted by Francisco Asorey in 1926. The barefooted saint stands in front of the crucified Jesus. Francis's hands are raised, displaying the same wounds as his Lord, for in 1224, while he was praying on a mountain in the Apennines, the five wounds which Jesus sustained when he was crucified appeared on the body of Francis himself. As for the church of San Francisco de Valdedios, it is said to have been founded in 1214, when the saint is alleged to have arrived at Compostela. A plaque in the lodge gives further false information. Francis, it says, stayed with a miner named Cotolay at the foot of the hill of Pedrosa. Each night the saint would pray on the mountainside, and there God ordered him to found a monastery in the valley of God and the Inferno (the *Val de Dios y Val del Infierno*, hence the name of the present monastery). Cotolay still sleeps in a tomb in the thirteenth-century chapter house of the convent he built. Over the centuries the church and monastery have been rebuilt, and today the church façade has a classical portico, flanked by two round columns and bearing a statue of Francis by José Ferreiro. A couple of classical towers, topped by cupolas, harmoniously complete its ensemble, the work of Melchor Prado Mariño in the 1780s.

I parked in the street of San Francisco beside the imposing façade of the university faculty of medicine, in order to explore the city on foot. Galicia had become extraordinarily wealthy in the sixteenth and seventeenth centuries, and much of this wealth was used to transform the face of the greatest pilgrimage centre in the whole of Spain in order to proclaim the glories of the Counter-Reformation. Yet though the city in consequence is, considered in its entirety, supremely a baroque masterpiece and to a lesser extend a Renaissance one, aspects of the Middle Ages continue to peep through. I hurried down the street to reach the fabulous cathedral, where this phenomenon of baroque overlying earlier architectural elements is abundantly displayed.

The street runs towards the cathedral between two of Santiago's most endearing buildings, the intimate Palacio del Gelmírez on the left and the sumptuous Hostal de los Reyes Católicos on the right. The first, one of Spain's finest civic buildings in the Romanesque style, was built in 1120 for the city's first archbishop, after a mob lusting in 1117 for the blood of the dictatorial Bishop Diego Gelmírez tore down his palace. The second, the Hospice of the Catholic Monarchs, was built on the orders of Ferdinand and Isabella of Spain after they had made their own pilgrimage to Compostela in 1496. They intended it as to house poor and sick pilgrims – ironically, for in 1954 it was transformed into a luxury hotel. Their architect was Enrique de Egas, chief surveyor of works at Toledo cathedral, and he devised a plan in which the hospice incorporated four huge patios and its own church (which has been transformed into a concert and exhibition hall). This hospice was finished by 1511. Its loveliest feature is its plateresque main doorway. Busts of Ferdinand and Isabella adorn the spandrels above the arch of the door. Between the double pilasters that flank this doorway are niches with statues of the naked Adam and Eve. Above Adam are fully clothed statues of St Catherine, St John the Baptist and St Peter, while above Eve rise St Lucia, St Elizabeth and St Paul. Next to St Paul is a statue of St James the Great, dressed as a pilgrim. On his right is Jesus himself, and the matching statues at the other side of the porch represent the Virgin Mary and St John the Evangelist.

Though not totally dominant in this sometime pilgrims' hospice, James puts in another appearance in the row of apostles above the main arch of the doorway. And above this arch is inscribed the proud legend *Magnus Fernandus et Grandis Helizabeth peregrinis divi Iacobi construi issere anno salutis MDI opus inchoatum decennio absolutum* ('Great Ferdinand and Great Isabella had this built for pilgrims of holy Santiago, a building begun in 1501 and finished within a decade').

The hospice rises on the north side of the plaza del Obradoiro, whose eastern flank is bordered by the cathedral. As a previous twentieth-century pilgrim (Elisabeth de Stroumillo) observed, today the sight of the plaza del Obradoiro in front of the cathedral is absurdly sensational. 'Ahead is the understated Romanesque façade of the college of S. Jerónimo; to the left the soaring cathedral façade; to the right the neo-classical 18th-century former seminary that houses the Town Hall, and immediately behind is the beautiful Plateresque front of the former pilgrims' hospice, now the luxury Hostál de los Reyes Catolicos.'

The cathedral façade is outrageously extravagant. Almost as soon as the cult of Santiago arose here, this cathedral needed rebuilding to accommodate the huge numbers of pilgrims who began to arrive. Seventeen bishops and most of the royal family came for its consecration in 899. The building, which like the present one boasted three naves, stood for fewer than a hundred years. In August 997 El Mansour sacked the city and demolished its cathedral. His horse drank from the Romanesque font which can still be seen in the present-day cathedral. Why did he not destroy the shrine of St James? One reason was perhaps the susceptibilities of the numerous Christian mercenaries in his army. The Arab historian Ibn Idhari tells a more touching tale. 'In Santiago,' he wrote, 'El Mansour found no one left save an old monk seated beside the tomb of the saint. "Why are you still here?" he asked him. "To do honour to St James," replied the monk, and the conqueror ordered that he should be left in peace.'

Bishop Pedro de Mezonzo began the rebuilding, but the present cathedral received its final shape only in the twelfth century, during forty years when the crafty and brilliant Diego Gelmírez was archbishop. Although passionately devoted to the cult of St James, Gelmírez was a prelate hated by many in Santiago, though when the city rose against him in 1117 it failed to topple him but managed to kill his brother. Amongst the most masterly of the many coups achieved by the archbishop was to persuade Alfonso VII to be crowned in his cathedral. Wholeheartedly supporting the monastic reforms emanating from the abbey of Cluny, Diego persuaded the Cluniac Pope Callixtus II to grant remarkable privileges to his cathedral. This house of God was now served by seventy-two canons, seven of which were cardinals. Gelmírez himself was made Papal Legate.

Diego's latest biographer tells well how the archbishop died. 'Would he last until Easter Day? Would he be able to preside with dignity, would he be able to preside at all, for the fortieth time, at the central festival of the Christian year?' wrote Richard Fletcher. 'Diego kept his attendants in suspense until the last possible moment. Then, with that flair for timing and publicity which had stood by him all his life, he ensured that even the Risen Christ would take a second place in the minds of those who celebrated Easter at Compostela that year. He died on Easter Eve, Saturday 6 April 1140.'

Unfortunately his death bought a temporary disruption in the fortunes of the cathedral. In the next thirty-three years no fewer than six archbishops succeeded him. There were long vacancies and many quarrels at Santiago; between clergy of the cathedral chapter, with the papacy, with the monarchy, with local nobles. The cathedral chapter ran out of money and building ceased. One canon named Pedro Marcio was driven to a brilliant piece of chicanery and forged the so-called Diploma of Ramiro I. Ramiro was king at the time of the battle of Clajivo in 844, and the fake charter decrees that in thanksgiving for the assistance of Santiago Matamoros at this victory, every part of Spain ruled by Christians should annually pay corn and wine to the chapter of Compostela cathedral and that the chapter should also receive a share of any booty captured from the Moors.

Because of these troubles Santiago cathedral, begun in 1074, was not consecrated until 1211. Work began again only when Pedro Suárez became archbishop in 1173. In the end the cathedral benefited enormously from the delay, for during the long reign of Pedro over the see of Compostela one of the finest examples of Spanish Romanesque art was added to the building, the famous Pórtico de la Gloria.

What is not immediately apparent is that you are looking at an essentially Romanesque cathedral. The churrigueresque west façade of the cathedral vibrates with wild ornamentation, balconies, pyramids, flowers and other excrescences. Its luxuriance gives the name to the plaza, for Obradoiro means work in gold. Fernando de Casas y y Nóvoa created this façade between 1738 and 1749. It is approached by way of a monumental double staircase of 1606. The belfry on the right rises from a Romanesque base, though you would scarcely guess this.

That on the left is called the tower of the rattle (*de la Carraca*) because of the wooden clapper it encloses, which is used to call the faithful to worship during Holy Week when the ringing of bells is forbidden. Standing in the plaza del Obradoiro you can see that the bell tower is leaning slightly out of true. Virtually the sole hint of the Romanesque are the statues of Moses and King David on either side of the parapet above the steps.

All this was built to the glory of St James. He stands in the niche at the top of the elaborate central arch, dressed as a pilgrim. Two monarchs kneel before him, while beneath his feet are sculpted his sarcophagus and the star which allegedly drew attention to his Spanish resting place. The statue in the niche on tower of the rattle re presents James's father Zebedee, while that in the niche on the bell tower represents Mary Salome, traditionally said to be his mother. The balconies in front of these towers carry four other statues, including St James the Less and his father St Alpheus.

Romanesque architecture at its most superb appears behind Fernando Casa y Novoa's façade. The Pórtico de la Gloria was finished by Master Mateo in 1178, its three doorways crammed with sculptures. Above the central doorway sits Jesus, displaying his wounds, supported by the four evangelists and censed by angels with thuribles. The eagle of St John perches quietly on his leg. St Luke's bull and St Mark's eagle sweetly put a leg over their masters' knees. Only St Matthew lacks a pet. Forty other figures stand for those Jews who accepted Jesus as the Messiah.

The archivolt is sculpted with the twenty-four elders of the Acopalypse, chattering away and having a rest from their virtually incessant duties as heavenly musicians, just as any performer behaves during an interval. Christian theology has the knack of turning the sufferings of Jesus into glory, and so one is not surprised to find sculpted at the base of the tympanum eight angels carrying the instruments of his passion: the pillar against which he was scourged; his cross; the crown of thorns; the reed that was mockingly put into his hand as a sign of royalty; a sponge which brought vinegar to his lips when he cried 'I thirst'; the cords with which he was whipped; the bowl in which Pontius Pilate tried to wash away responsibility for the crucifixion; a document bearing Jesus's death sentence; the lance that pierced his side; and the nails which fixed him to the cross.

Old Testament figures put in entertaining appearances. Adam tames two beasts; youthful, curly-haired Daniel beguilingly smiles at lithe Queen Esther; Moses and Isaiah and Jeremiah take their places. Their robes are marvellously delicate. The worthies of the New Testament depicted on the right of the doorway include St Peter, St Paul and St James the Less. In this brilliantly conceived doorway every inch of the space is covered with symbolic carvings. The left porch is devoted to the heroes of the Jewish faith. These gaze towards Jesus and their souls reach him in the form of babies. The right porch depicts the Last Judgement. Sculpted along with God the Father and God the Son are depictions of the seven cardinal virtues and the seven deadly sins. In a wry touch, gluttony is eating the traditional Galician pasty known as an *empanada*.

The mullion which supports this tympanum is sculpted with a tree of Jesse displaying the ancestry of Jesus and ending with the Holy Trinity and a depiction of Christ's temptations in the wilderness. Perched on it is St James the Great. He looks a little tired, barefoot, leaning on a T-shaped stick. His right hand holds a scrolll on which is inscribed *Missit me Dominus* ('The Lord sent me'). On this mullion is a quaint legacy of pilgrims: the incised mark of four fingers and a thumb, an impression made by millions who over the centuries have reverently placed their hands on this sacred spot. Pilgrims still do, and so did I. And Master Mateo carved an image of himself on the other side of the mullion, kneeling in prayer facing the high altar and recognizable by his lumpy hair. We know nothing about the master who created this gem of Romanesque architecture, and we only know his name and the date he finished the work (1188) from the inscription he left on the lintel of the central arch. Students of architecture used to knock their heads against his, to catch some of his brilliance.

Then they and the medieval pilgrim entered, as we do today, an early twelfth-century barrel-vaulted nave of a cathedral which is twenty-two metres high, ninety-four metres long and eighteen metres wide. The cupola of 1448 rises another ten metres from the crossing, for Santiago cathedral is in the shape of a Latin cross, whose wings stretch for another sixty-five metres. Its pattern is that of the great pilgrimage churches of France, particularly that found at St Sernin of Toulouse, and its predominant style remains Romanesque, with slender pillars upholding flattish round arches. But the strange essence of Santiago is never far away.

The tympanum of the south transept is adorned with a Romanesque image of Santiago Caballero, the vengeful saint leading the Spanish troops at the battle of Clajivo. Santiago looks out witheringly at you here, his toes in the stirrups of an exceedingly virile horse. Are the little figures whose hands are clasped in prayer beside him Moors begging mercy or the hundred Christian maidens asking to be rescued?

Looking east at the centre of the cathedral is a thrillingly theatrical experience. In a tremendous baroque baldacchino Santiago rides his charger brandishing his sword, a baroque fantasy of the sculptor Mateo de Prado. The baldacchino, built between 1658 and 1677, is the work of Domingo de Andrade, Bernardo de Cabrera and Francisco de Antas. Underneath this canopy stands St James in his pilgrim's hat, bearing his book and staff. Below this, guarded by rather fierce-looking cherubs, another statue of Santiago, carved in the Romanesque era and much embellished in later centuries, sits behind the high altar above the shrine where his bones are said to lie, his eyes staring fixedly ahead, his hair and beard close-cropped, his garments gilded.

I hurried down the steps to venerate not the statue but what I cannot think is the genuine relic. This crypt stands on the site of a first century AD Roman mausoleum. St James the Great is not alone here, for the remains of his two assistants, Theodore and Athanasius are said to lie with him. Kneeling before the neo-Romanesque reliquary, which was sensitively made in the Mudéjar style seventeen years after St James's bones had been rediscovered, I was joined by only one other person, a girl dressed in black, who began intently praying the rosary before the silver shrine.

There is much else of fascination in Santiago cathedral, and after all I had already seen I was surprised to discover a considerable amount still relating to St James. The westernmost chapel of the south aisle, which was built by Juan de Alava in 1527, serves both as the chapel of the relics and a royal pantheon. The relics in question include the head of St Alpheus, encased in a silver shrine. Evidently the whole of St James the Great is not preserved in the crypt, for here are two reliquaries enclosing parts of him, both the gift of Archbishop Alvaro de Isorna in 1449. On display too is a beautiful fourteenth-century statue of the saint as a pilgrim. An alabaster retable of 1456 depicts episodes from his life. It was the gift of an English pilgrim named John Gudjar. The sweetest scene is that where Jesus directs the fishermen-apostles to cast their nets into the sea for the umpteenth time. Meekly they obey.

Amongst the tombs housed in the pantheon here is that of Raymond of Burgundy, who died in 1107. He had married Urruca, the daughter of Alfonso IV, a marriage deliberately designed to strengthen the links between Compostela and Cluny, and he had become Count of Castile. Berenguela, Queen of Alfonso VII, died in 1149 and lies here too, rather mean-mouthed, I think, but still beautiful. As for King Ferdinand II of Léon, he was fortunate to die in 1188, precisely when Master Mateo was finishing the Pórtica de la Gloria, so that the royal remains repose in a tomb fashioned by Mateo himself. The king's hair and beard are exquisitely curly, his clothing is sinuous and he cups one hand to his ear while the other rubs his stomach. An honoured place in this royal pantheon has been given to Bishop Teodomiro of Iriense, who died in 847, for he it was who discovered the body of Santiago.

In the next chapel along this aisle I was delighted to see that the reliefs on the base of a mid-sixteenth-century processional monstrance include a scene in which the body of St James is being placed on a boat, ready to journey to Spain. Another scene depicts the miracle of Santo Domingo de la Calzada. Made by Antonio de Arfe, this complex masterpiece stands 1.75 metres high.

Similar treasures of metalwork and sculpture are housed in the other chapels of the cathedral. Amongst these chapels those in the apse alone preserve Romanesque elements in their design. The first one I reached from the south aisle does not. In 1711 this chapel of El Pilar was transformed by Domingo de Andrade and Bernardo de Cabrera into a pulsating baroque riot. Fernández de Sande sculpted the tomb of the Mexican Archbishop Antonio Monroy who paid for the transformation of this chapel and now lies there. The next chapel but one in the apse is still Romanesque. Dedicated to San Pedro, it was built between 1077 and 1102. Its altar was created in 1731 by the man who built the Obradoiro façade.

As for the chapel of El Salvador at the easternmost end of this deambulatory, it was consecrated by Diego Gelmírez in 1102 and enshirnes delicate Romanesque capitals on its columns. Latin inscriptions over the arch declare that it was built in the time of Prince Alfonso and Prelate Diego. Here multilingual priests would hear the confessions of foreign pilgrims, before handing them the certificate which proclaimed that they had successfully reached the pilgrimage goal. For this reason, perhaps, King Charles v of France gave an endowment to the chapel in 1380, and because of this the chapel of El Salvador is also known as the Capilla del Rey de Francia. Its colourful altarpiece clashes with the calm of the ancient stones. Finally, the next two chapels, that of Nuestra Señora de Blanca and of San Juan Apóstol, have both managed to remain coolly Romanesque in style.

At this corner of the cathedral is a curious addition to Santiago cathedral, the Corticela. Till it was taken under the wing of the cathedral in the seventeenth century the Corticela was an entirely separate church, built by Alfonso ii in the ninth century, and long run by Benedictine monks on behalf of foreign pilgrims. From here I walked back around the apse to stroll around the Gothic cloister which Juan de Alava began building in 1521. After his death in 1537 the work was taken over by Rodrigo Gil de Hontañon, hence the

Renaissance elements which start creeping into its architecture.

These long galleries of lovely vaulting abut on to another ex-quisite Romanesque survival, the Puerta de las Platerias, by which I left the cathedral. Puerta de las Platerias literally translated means the silversmiths' door, so-called because it opens out on to a square in-habited by silversmiths in the Middle Ages and still sheltering shops selling expensive silver cockle-shells. The double-arched doorway dates from the eleventh century. Above it are three arched windows, between two of which is a Romanesque Annunciation. Everything on the frieze above the door seems to my eyes to have been at one time taken down and then put back in a different way. St James appears there, among a couple of cypresses. The most delightful statue of all is that of King David, playing not a harp but a sort of gui-tar held upside-down, while foppishly crossing his slipper-clad feet. Of the rest I most relish the carving on the left tympanum depicting an adulterous woman. Dressed in diaphanous garments, she kisses her illicit lover's horrible skull.

I had not yet exhausted the riches of this flank of the cathedral. Next to the doorway the earliest clock-tower in Europe rises from a Romanesque tower of the cathedral. It was set up in 1552, though the present clock dates only from 1831. Nearby is the so-called Holy Door, opened only in a Holy Year, that is when the feast of St James falls on a Sunday. Those who managed to pass through it during such a year were granted such enormous indulgences from their sins that the door is also dubbed the Puerta del Pardón. Some of its twenty-four granite figures were carved by Master Mateo. Above this door, which is inevitably usually sealed, stands a benevolent St James in his pilgrim's guise. The niches below him house statues of his two com-panions, also dressed as pilgrims.

Walking back towards the plaza del Obradoiro past a fountain supported by prancing horses, I could not find him depicted any-where on the façade of the magical baroque chapter house which rises on the left; but his absence was more than compensated for by the huge scallops and the exuberant star carved on its parapet. I walked on to the Colegio San Jerónimo which flanks the south side of the plaza del Obradoiro. Built in 1662 as a college for poor students, it today houses the office of the university rectory. The seventeenth-century architects had the good sense to retain a Romanesque door-way from a former college, decorated with saints, angels and the Madonna. St James here is not altogether healthy, for although he re-tains his scrip, his nose and right hand have been knocked off. He re-gains his strength on the other building which closes off this superb square, the eighteenth-century Rajoy Palace. Now part of the town hall, this palace was commissioned by Archbishop Bartolomé Rajoy from a French architect named Chalres Lemaur. At the apex of its neo-classical façade, sculpted by José Ferreiro, Santiago Matamaros rides his charger and slices the head off another unfortunate Moor.

It was time to explore more of this city of narrow streets, monasteries with colonnaded cloisters, squares with unexpected arcades and palaces with convoluted balconies. One of Santiago de Compostela's most attractive features is the way the streets gently undulate. Still in search of St James, I found the church of San Martiño Panario, one of Santiago's most exuberant baroque buildings with a fabulous façade covered in cockle-shells. The statues it carries seem very grumpy. Although St Martin of Tours rightly has pride of place on the baldacchino inside the church, St James and his steed are here again. He puts in another wild appearance on the classical pinnacle of the Seminario Mayor (once the convent of San Martiño Panario) which rises beyond peaceful lawns. I discovered too the church dedicated to St James's mother, Santa Maria Salomé, which boasts a baroque tower and a Romanesque porch. In plaza del Toral I was entranced by the carving over the balcony of the Palacio de Bendaña of Atlas groaning under the weight of the globe.

In one of the most charming nooks of the city, the haphazard plaza de Mazarelos, which I reached by way of an ancient archway, I foolishly imagined that I had escaped St James's almost all-pervading presence. Here the former monastery of the Jesuits now serves as the university institute of philology, a huge coat of arms on its façade. On the opposite side of the square the houses are entrancing in part because of the different height of their roofs, their loggias and iron balconies. In the middle of the plaza rises a statue of the savant Eugenio Montero Rios, who (the plinth says) lived from 1832 to 1913. Here was no sign of St James, but just across the rúa de Caldereria rises the church and convent of Our Lady of Mercy. Above the Annunciation on its façade is a cockle-shell.

'Compostela, that most excellent city of the Apostle, which guards the precious body of St James, is full of every kind of delight,' wrote Aimery Picaud, 'and renowned as one of the happiest and most noble of all the cities of Spain.' His words remain true, and for centuries after he saw and described it, Santiago became increasingly magnificent. So, for example, the wife of Alfonso the Wise founded a convent for Franciscan nuns in 1260. Today the Franciscans are housed in a superb late-eighteenth century building by Pedro de Aren, its baroque façade designed by Simón Rodriques. A similar transformation overtook the convent of the Dominicans, which stands just outside the walls of Compostela, close by the Puerta del

Camiño. Founded by the passionate preacher St Domingo de Guz-
mán in the twelfth century, it now boasts a church of 1561 with a Renaissance façade, and the monastery also displays yet another
baroque façade, this one by none other than Domingo de Andrade.
Today the convent no longer houses monks but serves as the city
museum, which enabled me find my way inside to admire its superb
spiral staircase, another masterpiece by the same baroque genius.

I had hoped to arrive at Santiago de Compostela on Easter Day,
but failed. This was the Saturday after Easter. A pilgrimage, Hilaire
Belloc once observed, must not be untroublesome. 'On the way to
the grave of a saint of a man privately venerated for his virtues,' Belloc
insisted, 'the pilgrim must do something a little difficult to show at
what a price he holds communion with his resting place.' That evening I had to confess that my own pilgrimage to Compostela had been
scarcely troublesome. But Belloc added, 'also on the way I will see
what I can of men and things; for anything great and worthy is but an
ordinary thing transfigured, and if I am about to venerate a humanity
absorbed into the divine, so it behoves me on my journey to enter
into and delight in the divine that exists in everything.' I too had set
out hungry for real colours, for living men and women, for the feel of
architecture, hills and countryside, and had arrived sated.

The following morning I took a coffee in a café on whose tannoy
Gene Kelly was performing *Singing in the Rain* – appropriately, for
the rain was pouring down. The barman told me that it rains here
more than anywhere in Galicia, but that it often stops too. I did not
mind, for this was the Sunday after Easter and I went away to attend
Mass in the cathedral of my patron saint at Santiago de Compostela.
Standing there I, as surely countless English-speakers before me,
could scarcely fail to remember the opening lines of Sir Walter
Raleigh's *The Passionate Man's Pilgrimage*:

> Give me my scallop-shell of quiet,
> My staff of faith to walk upon,
> My scrip of joy, immortal diet,
> My bottle of salvatión,
> My gown of glory, hope's true gage:
> And thus I'll take my pilgrimage.

From a priest in the cathedral secretariat I obtained the certificate
stating that I had completed the pilgrimage. In past years these *com-
postelles* would have served to guarantee the papal pardon granted to
pilgrims, a pardon reputed to relieve them of half their time in purga-
tory. I had read that the *compostelle* still entitles a pilgrim to a free
meal at the Hostal de los Reyes Católicos across the plaza del Obra-

doiro, but felt too shy to go and check this. What I determined to do was return for the feast of Saint James, which in *éclat* outclasses the feast of the resurrection itself at Santiago de Compostela. Festivities begin in earnest on July 24th, the eve of the feast, with fireworks lighting up the façade of the cathedral and dancing in the plaza. At Mass on the feast day itself the largest censer in the world, the *botaf-umerio,* hanging from a pulley in the transept of the cathedral, is swung by six-red-robed acolytes, filling the building with the smoke and scent of burning incense. Then huge puppets appear again the square, pipes and drums set up their entertaining cacophany, the citizens don traditional costumes, some of them wearing masks and assortedly bizarre headgear, and in the evening Fernando de Casas y Novoa's churrigueresque façade is once again set off by fireworks, the porch of the cathedral glittering as it once did under the reds, blues, greens and gold-leaf of medieval artists.

GLOSSARY

Apse: the semicircular or sometimes polygonal termination of the east end of the choir or aisles of a church or cathedral.

Charles V: Grandson of the German emperor Maximilian I and son of the mad daughter of Ferdinand and Isabella of Spain, he became King Carlos I of Spain in 1517 and was elected Holy Roman Emperor two years later. Worn out by continual warfare and the intractable religious problems of a Europe he sought to dominate, he resigned his thrones in 1555, retired to a monastery in Estramadura and lived in seclusion till his death three years later.

Choir: that part of a church or cathedral set apart for the celebration of services by the priests and canons; usually situated at the east end, but in many Spanish cathedrals set in the centre of the building and protected by an ornate screen.

Churrigueresque: an extremely ornate fashion of baroque architecture, deriving its name from José de Churriguera (1665-1723) but carried to greater extremes of lavishness by his successors and seen at its finest in the west façade of the cathedral of Santiago de Compostela.

Cid, El: The title (from the Moorish *Sidi*, which means 'my lord') applied to the legendary Spanish champion Rodrigo Diáz de Vivar (c. 1043-1099) who, though at times willing to offer his services as a mercenary to the Moors, helped to reconquer parts of Spain from them, in particular retaking Valencia in 1094.

Confraternity: a group of lay Christians, organised both for religious observances (particularly those of Holy Week) and for such charitable activities as burying the dead.

Deambulatory: a 'space for walking', applied particularly to the sanctuary of a church is surrounded by continuous aisles, so that worshippers are enabled to visit a series of chapels built around the apse and ceremonial processions can follow the same progress; also known as an ambulatory.

Hermitage: a religious sanctuary usually isolated in the countryside.

Mozarabic: appertaining to Christians in Spain under Muslim rule, who were allowed to practise their religion provided that they paid tribute to their masters.

Mudéjar: appertaining to Muslims in Spain under Christian rule, and in particular to their work as architects on behalf of the Christians.

Plateresque: delicate and intricate surface decoration of renaissance architecture, so called because of its resemblance to the work of goldsmiths *(plateros)* and developed in Spain above all by Diego de Siloé (c. 1495-1563), a French sculptor who made his home at Burgos.

Reliquary: a chest of casket to hold the bodies (or parts of the bodies) of saints.

Retable: a painting or sculpture set behind an altar; also known as a reredos.

Sanctuary: the eastern end of the choir of a church or cathedral, housing the high altar.

Sedilia: the Latin for 'seat', applied in particular to those on the south side of a church or cathedral altar for the use of the priest and his attendants.

BIBLIOGRAPHY

Alcolea, Ramón *La Catedral de Santiago*, Editorial Plus-Ultra, Madrid, n.d.

Bernadac, Jean *Les Chemins Saint Jacques en Vendômois*, L'Imprimerie de Val de Loire, s.a., Thoré-le-Rochette, 1988.

Bernès, Georges, Veron, Georges and Balen, Louis Laborde *Le Chemin de Saint Jacques de Compostelle*, Éditions randonnées pyrénées, 2nd edition 1989.

Billard, Michel *Sur les pas des Pélerins de Saint-Jacques de Compostelle*, Éditions du Soleil natal, Étampes, 1989.

Bishop, Hal The Way of Saint James, Cicerone press, Milnthorpe, Cumbria, 1989.

Bécet, Maurice *Vézelay*, Éditions Alpina, Paris, n.d.

Bottineau, Yves *Les Chemins de Saint-Jacques*, Arthaud, Paris 1983.

Bourdarias, Jean and Wasielewski, Michel *Guide des Chemins de Compostelle*, Librairie Arthène Fayard, Rennes 1989.

Brooke, Rosalind and Christopher *Popular Religion in the Middle Ages*, Thames and Hudson, 1984.

Chamoso Lamas, Manuel 'El altar del Apóstel en la Catedral de Santiago', in *Boletin de la Commisión Provincial de Monumentos de Oresne*, vol. XI, enero-febrero 1937, pp.266ff.

Clissold, Stephen 'Saint James in Spanish History', in *History Today* October 1975, pp.684-692.

Conant, Kenneth John *The Early Architectural History of Santiago de Compostela*, Harvard University Press, Cambridge, Massachusetts, 1926.

Duchesne, L. 'S. Jacques en Galice,' in *Annales du Midi*, tôme xii, 1900, pp.145-180.

Fletcher, R. A. *Saint James's Catapult. The Life and Times of Diego Gelmirez of Santiago de Compostela*, O.U.P., Oxford 1984.

Hartley, Catherine G. *The Story of Santiago de Compostela*, J. M. Dent, 1912.

Hell, Vera and Helmut *The Great Pilgrimage of the Middle Ages. The Road to St. James of Compostela*, translated by Alisa Jaffa, Barrie and Rockliff, 1964.

T. D. Kendrick *St James in Spain*, Methuen & Co., 1060.

Layton, T. A. *The Way of Saint James*, George Allen and Unwin, 1976.

Lomax, Derek W. *La Orden de Santiago*, Consejo Superior de Investigaciones Científicas, Madrid, 1965.

Marshall-Cornwall, James 'The Myth of Santiago', in *History Today*, March 1981, pp.46f.

Meurgey, Jacques *Histoire de la Paroisse Saint-Jacques-de-la-Boucherie,* Champion, Paris 1926.

Mullins, Edwin *The Pilgrimage to Santiago,* Secker and Warburg, 1974.

Neillands, Rob *The Road to Compostela,* Moorlands Publishing Co. Ltd., Ashbourne 1984.

Pedrayo, Ramón Otera *Santiago de Compostela,* Editorial Noguera, S.A., Barcelona, 1958.

Oursel, Raymond and Jean-Nesmy, Claude *Les Chemins de Compostelle,* Zodiaque, Paris 1989.

Porter, A. Kingsley *Romanesque Sculpture of the Pilgrim Roads,* Marshall Jones Company, Boston 1923.

Secret, Jean *Saint-Jacques et les Chemins de Compostelle,* Horizons de France, Paris 1955.

Starkie, Walter *The Road to Santiago,* John Murray, 1957.

Stroumillo, Elisabeth de *The Tastes of Travel. Northern and Central Spain,* Collins and Harvill Press, 1980.

Urrutibéhety, Clément *Jonction des Chemins de St-Jacques en Basse-Navarre et en Navarre,* Communication au ler Congrès Général d'Histoire de Navarre, Saint-Palais, 1986.

USEFUL ADDRESSES

The Confraternity of St. James,
57 Leopold Road,
London N2 8BG
Telephone: 081 883 4893

Tourist Office,
Rúa del Villar, 43,
Santiago de Compostela
Spain
Telephone: 58 40 81

French Government Tourist
Office,
178 Piccadilly,
London W1V 0AL
Telephone: 071 493 6911

Spanish National Tourist Office,
57 St. James's Street,
London SW1 1LD
Telephone: 071 499 0901

Index